LITERARY PORTRAITS IN THE NOVELS OF HENRY FIELDING

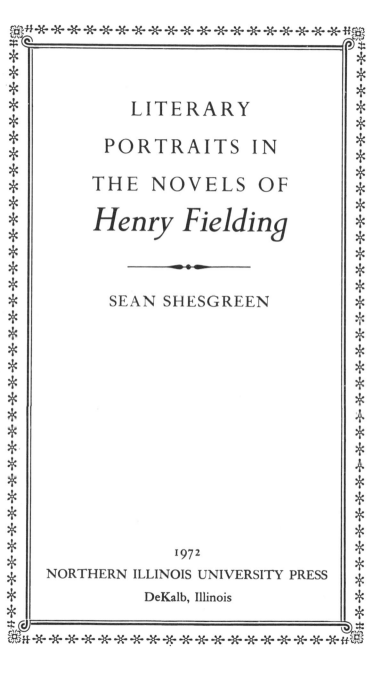

LITERARY
PORTRAITS IN
THE NOVELS OF
Henry Fielding

SEAN SHESGREEN

1972
NORTHERN ILLINOIS UNIVERSITY PRESS
DeKalb, Illinois

Library of Congress Cataloging in Publication Data
Shesgreen, Sean, 1939–
    Literary portraits in the novels of Henry Fielding
    Bibliography: p.
        1. Fielding, Henry, 1707–1754.   2. Characters and
    characteristics in literature.   I. Title.
PR3457.S5   823'.5   72–1389
ISBN 0–87580–029–7

TO
JEAN HAGSTRUM
AND
MARY SHESGREEN

Contents

Preface / ix
Introduction / 3

1. Background / 10
2. Jonathan Wild / 45
3. Joseph Andrews / 7?
4. Tom Jones / 106
5. Amelia / 154

Conclusion / 177
Notes / 180
Bibliography / 192
Index / 201

Preface

IN MY LABORS on this book I was assisted by a summer grant from the College of Arts and Sciences at Northern Illinois University; I am thankful to the College and the English Department for their support. The staff at Northwestern University's Dearing Library, where I began my work, assisted me generously. My debt is great to Art Miller and his associates who made the full facilities of the Newberry Library available for the early stages of research. I am happy to acknowledge the hospitality offered by Dr. Patrick Henchey and his staff at the National Library, Dublin. Part of chapter 4 appeared in a somewhat different form in *Studies in the Novel* (summer, 1970), and I thank the editors for permission to reprint it here.

Among those individuals who assisted in this work, I wish to thank my mother for her encouragement, Judy Lawson for her inspiration and stimulation, Dona Ruby for her editorial wisdom, and Sue Dahl for help in preparing the manuscript. I am especially grateful to Professors Don Torchiana and Robert Mayo for reading the manuscript and offering sensitive, helpful suggestions.

My greatest debt is to Professor Jean H. Hagstrum, whose encouragement and direction have been as constant as they have been valuable. Mary Shesgreen's labors on early versions of this study have been almost as great as mine; her wisdom, penetration, and generosity have contributed much to the work. Without the assistance of both these people, this study could not have been written.

No complete edition of Fielding's works is presently available; happily, Clarendon Press and Wesleyan University Press are currently engaged in establishing an authoritative text of the entire Fielding canon. In this study, therefore, it has been necessary to cite a variety of editions employing different styles of capitalization and punctuation. The principal editions cited in this book are listed below.

> *Joseph Andrews*, ed. Martin Battestin (Middletown, Conn., 1967).
>
> *Tom Jones*, ed. R. P. C. Mutter (Baltimore, 1966).
>
> *The Covent-Garden Journal*, ed. Gerard E. Jensen (2 vols.; New Haven, 1915).

Unless otherwise stated, quotations from Fielding's other works are from: *The Complete Works of Henry Fielding*, ed. William E. Henley (New York, 1902). Citations from the *Greek Anthology* and Fielding's works are identified immediately after the quotations. For the convenience of readers who may not have the cited editions of the novels at hand, the arabic numerals indicate the book and chapter numbers of the excerpts. References to other works of Fielding are cited by the volume and page numbers of the Henley edition.

Abbreviations of periodical titles, used in the footnotes and bibliography, are the same as used in the *Publications of the Modern Language Association* annual bibliography.

Letterkenny, Donegal   S.N.S.

August 10, 1971

LITERARY PORTRAITS IN THE
NOVELS OF HENRY FIELDING

Introduction

I

T IS NOT SURPRISING that artists of the neoclassic period, committed to the study of mankind, devoted so much energy to formal portraiture. In Samuel Butler's prose, in Dryden's and Pope's poetry, in the *Tatler* and *Spectator* essays, in Johnson's *Lives*, in the engravings of Hogarth, and in the paintings of Reynolds and Gainsborough character portraits hold an important or a dominant place. Among the major eighteenth-century novelists, no one made more use of literary portraiture than Henry Fielding, whose novels abound with a variety of interesting verbal portraits. In his four novels there are over thirty major portraits and countless minor sketches (two or three sentences in length); they range from the pithy, ethical sketches in *Jonathan Wild* through the lengthy portraits in *Joseph Andrews* and *Tom Jones* (the portrait of Sophia runs a whole chapter) to the graphic, Hogarthian delineations in the opening of *Amelia*.[1]

The designations "literary portraiture" and "literary portrait" have been used by critics for any sketch or drawing of fictional characters, so that it seems appropriate to define these terms more closely before proceeding with this investigation. Literary portraiture may be divided into two kinds, indirect and direct. Indirect portraiture depicts character by dramatic techniques, that is, by means of dialogue and the action of the plot. Direct portraiture presents character by picturing appearance or by describing (and sometimes evaluating) disposition or ethos by means of statements about moral and psychological traits, and it usually combines these approaches. Unlike indirect portraiture, which leaves inference and evaluation to the reader, direct portraiture (sometimes referred to as "set-piece characterization") involves authorial intervention, and so it usually employs a pause in narration and is often bounded and static in nature.

This study is concerned primarily with direct portraiture. It uses "literary portrait" to describe any formal depiction of character that offers the reader a visual impression of a figure's physical appearance, a moral and psychological analysis, an evaluation of disposition, or a combination of these. Indirect literary portraiture will be considered only when actions and events are consciously and formally organized to suggest a person.[2]

Concerned with the art of Fielding's literary portraiture, we propose to isolate and comment upon the important sketches in his novels, to discover the main influences and traditions behind the portraits and, for the modern reader, to establish the conventions associated with these backgrounds. This inquiry also proposes to classify the sketches according to the literary traditions from which they derive, to analyze their structure, and to identify the nature and function of the principal techniques they employ. In discussing these problems the study will inquire into matters of tone, diction, imagery, convention, and purpose. Questions of larger scope will also be raised: we will examine the place of the individual portraits in the overall design of the novels. Finally, we will chart the development or change in Fielding's craft as he moved from the inherited, classical forms to newer, more experimental techniques. By means of this analysis and commentary, the study hopes to demonstrate the importance and vitality of literary portraiture in Fielding's novels.

This work makes no effort to match Fielding's characters with historical figures in his circle of friends and enemies. Such identifications are generally tentative at best—witness the controversies over Fielding's real-life source for Square.[3] The value of these identifications, even when they are unassailable, is questionable.

In Alexander Pope's poetry it is important that we match particular historical personages with the figures in his character sketches. Usually, Pope is attacking or praising individuals, and only indirectly the type or class they represent. The reverse is true in Fielding's writings; the novelist was concerned almost exclusively with types ("I describe not Men, but Manners; not an Individual, but a Species"). He eschewed traits which would identify his figures with contemporaries, aware that such associations could distract his readers from the general reach of his satire and dissipate the power and force of his *exempla*.

Fielding himself summarized his position and the case against identification in the preface to *Joseph Andrews*:

> I have no Intention to vilify or asperse any one: for tho'
> every thing is copied from the Book of Nature, and
> scarce a Character or Action produced which I have
> not taken from my own Observations and Experience,

> yet I have used the utmost Care to obscure the Persons
> by such different Circumstances, Degrees, and Colours,
> that it will be impossible to guess at them with any de-
> gree of Certainty.

Not to be misinterpreted as a facetious disclaimer about
actual attacks on contemporaries in *Joseph Andrews*, this
statement is in harmony with his general conception of
character as "typical" and it describes an important aspect
of his aesthetic.

It may be thought that an apology is necessary for con-
sidering so many of Fielding's characters outside the context of their novels, but such an approach is suggested by
the traditions of the character sketch. Literary portraits,
from ancient times down to Fielding's day, were used to
enliven and amplify long compositions.[4] They were literary creations or set pieces that retained independence
within the larger work because of their autonomous form
and ornamental function. Fielding was aware of this
traditional use of the literary portrait and in his remarks on
David Simple (quoted below) he compared sketches in
his sister's novel to the independent character studies of
Theophrastus, Horace, and La Bruyere. Indeed, his practice and commentary in his own novels make it plain that
he was writing from similar assumptions.

Still, it seems desirable to reduce the heightened sense
of isolation that inevitably arises when characters are
treated apart from their settings. Consequently, figures
will be considered not in the broad categories in which
they are classified but within the context of their appropriate novels. Furthermore, the settings in which they
are introduced will be investigated and the relationships
between figures will be considered.

Because Fielding was a dramatist for almost ten years before he became a novelist it has been suggested that the characters in his novels come from the drama, and particularly from his comedies of manners—and indeed he carried over many important techniques of characterization from his plays. Dialogue, of course, is a dramatic technique and his novels are full of imaginative, clever uses of it. Quirks of behavior to provide entertainment and to identify characters also seem to have come from the drama.[5] Only one class of characters, however, can be traced to the drama without much fear of contradiction.[6] These figures, called "situation characters," are formulated by reference to a single trait, are given self-judging, humorous names, and play only minor, supporting roles in the novels.[7] They include such people as Tom Thimble, Jack Ostler, Friendly, Bondum, Justice Frolick, Tittle, Tattle, Suckbribe, Straddle, and Swagger.

It cannot be denied that many of the important types in Fielding's novels may be found in contemporary drama. Figures like the superannuated coquette, the attractive hero, the lawyer, beau, maid servant, and doctor are common to both genres.[8] But the same types are found in many other literary forms, from the character book to satiric poetry, and each of these genres may claim some measure of influence on Fielding's characterization. It is not impossible to adjudicate these rival claims; a detailed and highly discriminating genealogical investigation of specific type characters could undoubtedly reveal a great deal about the sources for and influences on the figures in the novels. But because such a study is outside the scope of this work, questions of pedigree and lineage will generally be avoided.[9]

II

While Fielding scholarship has not failed to recognize literary portraits as part of the novelist's technique of characterization, too much stress has been put on the importance of dialogue as a means of characterization because of an overemphasis on the influence of Fielding's early career as a dramatist. Misconception has also arisen from the inevitable comparison with Richardson, in which the latter is praised for his intense character analysis while Fielding is admired for the way in which he manipulates his complex plot and action, frequently in the service of characterization. Consequently, most Fielding critics in the early part of this century have emphasized dramatic devices as the principal elements of the novelist's character presentation while ignoring his literary portraits. With few exceptions, they have observed little significance in the novelist's psychological analysis and physical descriptions and have felt, with the authors of *The History of the Novel in England*, that, "slightly analyzed by the author, Fielding's . . . persons reveal themselves through their speech and actions."[10]

George Saintsbury, for example, made no comment on Fielding's character sketches; he seemed to limit the novelist's means of characterization to a single mode when he claimed that Fielding "recognises the efficacy of dialogue as the revealer of character."[11] Wilbur Cross, in his *Development of the English Novel*, took much the same position on Fielding's characterization, stressing the immediate relevance of the drama to the novel.[12] He asserted that all the novels are dramatic and that "all his characters are constructed on a further development of the art of the comic dramatist."[13] Naturally, he felt that the novels' most important means of characterization are dramatic: "Character is unfolded . . . by direct, not reported, conversations."[14] Cross mentioned no other techniques of depiction. Ernest Baker, however, was careful to point out, in his discussion of Fielding, that "descriptive portraiture" is one of the novelist's means of characterization.[15] Yet he pointed to only a few examples (all in *Joseph Andrews*), and dismisses them. "But it is not by mere description, it is by making his characters speak and act that he puts them before us; and here Fielding has a knack of making them bare their inmost selves, expose their essential traits in the first few syllables uttered. The character-drawing, in short, is in the dialogue itself."[16]

Recent critics have been more sensitive to Fielding's character drawing. The work of scholars like Douglas Brooks, John S. Coolidge, Martin Battestin, Morris Golden, and William J. Farrell (among others) has done much to increase our awareness of the novelist's literary portraiture.[17] Yet, despite the labors of these men, the importance and richness of Fielding's portraiture are not generally recognized, and work in this area is only beginning. This study is an attempt to build on the scholarship of these critics. It proposes to examine the literary, visual, mythological, and emblematic aspects of Henry Fielding's direct characterization. By this examination, it aims to reveal the richness and complexity of Fielding's work and thereby contribute to an even, undistorted appreciation of his achievement in the presentation of character.

CHAPTER ONE

Background

HE CHARACTERS in Fielding's novels are numerous and diverse but the methods by which they are presented are relatively few. Four different traditions or methods of depicting figures can easily be distinguished: characters are usually described by means of (I) biographical character sketches, (II) psychological or moral character sketches, (III) idealized portraits, and (IV) portrait caricatures. This chapter will examine the backgrounds and most important characteristics of each of these descriptive procedures.

I

The "great man" in *Jonathan Wild* is presented at some length in the opening chapters, whose headings indicate the method by which the reader is introduced to the "hero":

> Chapter I. Showing the wholesome uses drawn from recording the achievements of those wonderful productions of nature called Great Men.
> Chapter II. Giving an account of as many of our hero's ancestors as can be gathered out of the rubbish of

antiquity, which hath been carefully sifted for that purpose.

Chapter III. The birth, parentage, and education of Mr. Jonathan Wild the Great.

Chapter IV. Mr. Wild's first entrance into the world. His acquaintance with Count La Ruse.

In *Joseph Andrews*, Joseph is also described at the very opening of the novel. Again, the chapter title tells us how the hero is to be introduced: "Of Mr. *Joseph Andrews* his Birth, Parentage, Education, and great Endowments, with a Word or two concerning Ancestors." The forms of these two descriptions are tellingly alike; both miniature biographies treat the same subjects in the same sequence. This use of identical topics and similar chronology is not accidental: behind the presentation of these figures, guiding the novelist in the invention and organization of his material, is a formula from classical rhetoric books which was a common tool in character drawing and biography with writers down to Fielding's day.[1]

This formula, known simply as "praise and blame" (more commonly as *laus et vituperatio*), was discussed in all standard rhetoric books, beginning with Aristotle and continuing through the Renaissance to the eighteenth century, but the function of the praise-and-blame formula was conceived in a number of ways. In Thomas Wilson's *Arte of Rhetorique* (1560), for example, it was recommended as a device for structuring a demonstrative oration in praise or dispraise of an individual.[2] For such an oration, and for any other literary form with similar ends, Wilson's book (and almost all other rhetorics) provides a list of topics or informational categories that could be applied to any subject. No distinction is made between topics for praise and topics for blame, so that the possibilities for ambiguity are unlimited. There is little variation in the number and nature of those categories from one book to another. Quintilian's *Institutes of Oratory*, Richard Sherry's *A Treatise of Schemes and Tropes* (1550), and Wilson's *Arte of Rhetorique* all contain the same basic "places" for the orations of praise and blame.

Richard Rainolde's *The Foundacion of Rhetorike* (1563)—an English adaptation of Aphthonius's fourth-century *Progymnasmata*—contains a typical discussion of *laus et vituperatio*.[3] It is of special interest here because schoolboys at Eton were required to follow either Aphthonius or Hermogenes as guides in composition.[4]

> This parte of Rhetorike called praise, is either a particuler praise of one, as of kyng Henry the fifte, Plato, Tullie, Demosthenes, Cyrus, Darius, Alexander the greate.
>
> Or a generalle and universalle praise, as the praise of all the Britaines: or of all the citezeins of London.
>
> The order to make this Oracion is thus declared.
>
> Firste, for the enteryng of the matter, you shall place a exordium, or beginnyng.
>
> The seconde place, you shall bryng to his praise, Genus eius, that is to saie: Of what kinde he came of, whiche dooeth consiste in fower pointes.
> > Of what nacion.
> > Of what countree.
> > Of what auncetours.
> > Of what parentes.
>
> After that you shall declare, his educacion; the educacion is conteined in three pointes.
> > In $\begin{cases} \text{Institucion.} \\ \text{Arte.} \\ \text{Lawes.} \end{cases}$

Then put there to that, whiche is the chief grounde of al praise: his actes doen, which doe procede out of the giftes, and excellencies of the minde, as the fortitude of the mynde, wisdome, and magnanimitee.

Of the bodie, as a beautifull face, amiable countenaunce, swiftenesse, the might and strength of the same.

The excellencies of fortune, as his dignitee, power, authoritee, riches, substaunce, frendes.

In the fifte place use a comparison, wherein that whiche you praise, maie be advaunced to the uttermoste.

Laste of all, use the Epilogus, or conclusion.[5]

This outline is followed by an illustration in which all these categories or topics are applied, and "blame" is rendered in the same manner.

Thomas Vicars's exposition of this subject in his orthodox survey of classical theory, *Manductio ad Artem Rhetoricana* (1721), shows how little the treatment of praise and blame had changed in Fielding's day. A commonplace textbook in the eighteenth century, this rhetoric was studied and even memorized by ordinary schoolboys on the elementary level. By means of a question-and-answer method, Vicars's book provides a fairly comprehensive treatment of the form and matter of a panegyrical composition:

Quinam est primus locus?
 Natio, Graecus ne sit an Barbarus, Gallus, an Anglus.
Quinam est secundus?
 Patria, Romanus ne sit an Bononiensis, Londinensis
  an Oxoniensis habent enim urbes propria instituta,
  mores, leges. . . .
Tertius?

Genus seu natales, maiores, parentes, propinqui si sint
splendidi, nobiles, honesti.
Quartus?
Sexus. Aliae virtutes in muliere, aliae in viro com-
mendantur.
Quintus?
Nomen proprium, quod aliquando peculiaris cuius-
piam rei admonet.[6]

This rhetorical formula, fundamental to many different
types of writing, has acquired a variety of associations
from its uses. It was employed most frequently in serious
histories and biographies, both classical and modern.
Plutarch used the biographical character sketch in his lives
of Alexander and Cicero. The form is also used in Suetonius's *De Vita Caesarum* and in the biographical writings
of Nepos and Diogenes Laertius. The early churchmen
also used it in their writings. The static formula is so well
suited to depicting a generalized, representative, ethical
figure and the topics or places so invite the narration of
prodigies that this method became a universal guide for
writing the lives of the saints.[7] At one point, *laus* was a
synonym for hagiography.[8]

In Fielding's period, *laus et vituperatio* was used in
both serious and satiric literature, particularly as a method
of beginning biographies. Middleton's *Cicero* (much
maligned by Fielding) and Walton's *Lives* begin with a
discussion of ancestry, parentage, and education. Even
the epic, the genre Fielding allies his novels with, was considered a form of *laus* (as "a panegyric biography") and
the formula for praise was believed to pertain to it.[9] At
the other end of the spectrum, Mr. Spectator used this
device humorously in his introductory autobiographical

essay, and Martin Scriblerus employed many of its topics
satirically in his *Memoires*.[10]

The importance of history and biography and the for-
mulas and conventions of these forms have not been
adequately recognized in Fielding's novels. There is persuasive evidence that he had extensive acquaintance with
these narrative types before *Jonathan Wild* had taken
shape in his mind and before *Joseph Andrews* was even
conceived.[11] In an essay in *The Champion* (4 February
1739/40) he claimed: "I have read most of the ancient
and modern Historians." His frequent references to biographers and historians confirm this claim, as do the contents of his library. According to the sale catalogue of
Fielding's library, he owned the works of Nepos, Caesar,
Terence, and Suetonius, a large collection of ecclesiasti-
cal biographies, and several editions of Izaak Walton's
Lives. Except for the ancients, history and biography
came close to law in the number of titles in his library.[12]
Finally, the titles of Fielding's novels, which (with the
exception of *Amelia*) contain the key words "history"
or "life," words characteristic of this rhetorical and
biographical tradition, indicate his familiarity with, and
imitation of, the biographical character sketch as it appeared abstractly in rhetorical books and as it was employed in classical and contemporary biography and
history.[13]

II

In the preface to the second edition of *David Simple*
(1744) Fielding gives a brief critical appreciation of the
characters in his sister's novel:

As to the Characters here described, I shall repeat the

Saying of one of the greatest Men of this Age, That they are wonderfully drawn by the Writer, as they were by *Nature* herself. *There are many Strokes in* Orgueil, Spatter, Varnish, Le-vif, *the* Balancer *and some others, which would have shined in the Pages of* Theophrastus, Horace, *òr* La Bruyere.[14]

It would seem from this quotation, and from Fielding's own practice, that he felt the "Theophrastan" character was directly related to the character in the novel and was relevant to a discussion of the novel's fictional persons. Although most modern critics have agreed with him, none of them has made a close analysis of the nature of this complex relationship. This section therefore outlines the traditions in character writing with which Fielding was familiar and it attempts to determine the novelist's relationship to this genre and its characteristics.

The character sketch is defined by William G. Crane as "a concise representation by means of vivid and concrete yet prominently distinctive details, selected to make a generic picture."[15] The two most important branches of character writing in England during Fielding's time were the Theophrastan sketch (in translation) and the native English sketch. Although "Theophrastan character sketch" is used above to refer to both branches of this genre, from this point on the term will refer only to the work of the Greek philosopher and "English character sketch" will designate the work of such seventeenth-century English character writers as Joseph Hall, Sir Thomas Overbury, and John Earle. It is impossible to enumerate all the characteristics of these two major classes and their subdivision; however, a working distinction will be adequate for our purposes.

The Theophrastan character is not a subtle creation.[16]

It is generally based on a broad moral quality and "Arrogance," "Petty Pride," "Meanness," "Flattery," and "Newsmaker" are representative of the type. The sketch begins by naming and defining an immoral quality and the substance of the sketch is a mechanical recital of actions and speech considered to be the natural and typical manifestations of this vice. The emphasis is exclusively on the description of operative character; that is, examples of speech and action are formally organized to illustrate a single moral abstraction. (Depiction by illustrative action and speech, a central characteristic of the Theophrastan sketch, will be called "dramatic characterization" in this study. Depiction by motives, thoughts, mental traits, and inclinations—the distinguishing technique of the English sketch—will be termed "psychological characterization.") No attention is paid to individuating qualities in the Theophrastan sketch; only universal and nonparticular actions are represented In the entire range of characters, only vices or extremes (with virtue residing implicitly in the *via media*) are presented. A student of Aristotle, Theophrastus created his figures around that philosopher's doctrine of the mean.

The native English character sketch in the seventeenth and eighteenth centuries departs from its classical model in many important ways. This branch is as much the product of training in rhetoric as a result of the influence of specific character books, and it is important to know that Fielding's initial and formative interest in this genre may have been generated by the rhetorical training he received at Eton. The characteristic qualities of the native genre are contained in the following rules for "making" a character—from Ralph Johnson's *The Scholars Guide from the Accidence to the University*[17] (1655):

A character is a witty and facetious description of the nature and qualities of some person, or sort of people.
1. Chuse a Subject, viz. such a sort of men as will admit of variety of observation, such be, drunkards, usurers, lyars, taylors, excise-men, travellers, pedlars, merchants, tapsters, lawyers, an upstart gentleman, a young Justice, a Constable, an Alderman, and the like.
2. Express their natures, qualities, conditions, practices, tools, desires, aims, or ends, by witty Allegories, or Allusions, to things or terms in nature, or art. . . .
3. Conclude with some witty and neat passage, leaving them to the effect of their follies or studies.[18]

From the examples Johnson gives it is clear that the native character, while remaining fundamentally moral in orientation, is also founded on psychological, occupational, ethical, and class bases. Like the Theophrastan sketch, it employs description of action ("practices"); however, its development also depends on "the nature and qualities of some person," that is, on psychological methods of characterization: the description of thoughts, sentiments, inclinations, qualities of mind, traits, and stable mental dispositions. Occasionally, a character is described in detail (but never by visual or physical description). However, even in such cases the emphasis is still on the typical and universal, if to a lesser degree than in Theophrastus's work, where the focus is constantly on the vice rather than on the human type. From the beginning, English character books describe both good and bad types rather than the Aristolian extremes of evil. The very first, Joseph Hall's work, is titled *Characters of Vertues and Vices* (1608).

In the English familiar essay the character took on a slightly different form. The best-known and most sophisticated development of character in the periodicals is found in the *Spectator,* and in the second issue there were sketches of the six characters who were intimates of Mr. Spectator. These sketches are of types that were chosen and fashioned to represent important classes and occupations in eighteenth-century English life, and there are substantial differences between these figures and those in the character books. The fictional people in the essays (described by psychological and dramatic methods) are differentiated by class and disposition. They relate to each other in social and economic terms—not as moral or psychological personifications in strict, didactic antithesis. In general, the *Spectator* portraits are more particularized than the highly abstract figures in the character books.

In works like Earle's *Micro-Cosmographie,* particularity is consistently excluded to protect the sketches' generic purity. In the *Spectator* sketches, however, characters' idiosyncrasies are emphasized; their residence is assigned to specific localities (Worcestershire or Soho, for example); and most are given names (Sir Roger de Coverly, Sir Andrew Freeport, Captain Sentry, Will Honeycomb) which, however significant, are considerably more subtle than the names of figures in the influential comedy of manners. The many attempts to identify the *Spectator* characters with contemporaries of the essayists are the strongest testimony to this emphasis on particularity. And while the represented types are never "obscured" by individuating marks, it is evident from the lavish attention to descriptive detail that the individuality of the characters is only a little less important than their typicality.

Fielding knew all these literary forms, which influenced his depiction of persons, and indications of these traditions in his novels may be observed in various aspects of his characterization. Boyce has shown that the word "character" at the introduction of a sketch is adequate evidence of the genre in what follows. This superficial but telling clue is not hard to find in Fielding's novels. In *Jonathan Wild* he introduces the Heartfrees under the heading "Characters of silly people," and the book concludes with a chapter titled "The character of our hero." In *Tom Jones* we are given "the Character of Mrs Western," "a short Sketch of the Characters of two Brothers," and many more "characters." Fielding is so devoted to this tradition that he even employed it in a little-used form to give us the "character" of a house.

The art comprehended here by the word "character"—of describing or summarizing a figure in a literary form that is bounded and static—is an important part of Fielding's portraiture. This method of fixing a type or personality in a vividly intellectual and abstract description is, of course, the essential method of the character books. So, too, is the practice of establishing relationships between characters in ethical patterns and creating characters as personifications of vices and virtues, which also are important aspects of the art of Fielding's literary portraiture.

III

Two other methods of character description, outside the traditions just discussed, also operate in Fielding's novels—one of which is typified in the elaborate description of Fanny in *Joseph Andrews*. Her literary portrait also invites scrutiny because it contains the pattern for the description of a number of Fielding's major characters.

Fanny was now in the nineteenth Year of her Age; she was tall and delicately shaped; but not one of those slender young Women, who seemed rather intended to hang up in the Hall of an Anatomist, than for any other Purpose. On the contrary, she was so plump, that she seemed bursting through her tight Stays, especially in the Part which confined her swelling Breasts. Nor did her Hips want the Assistance of a Hoop to extend them. The exact Shape of her Arms, denoted the Form of those Limbs which she concealed; and tho' they were a little redden'd by her Labour, yet if her Sleeve slipt above her Elbow, or her Handkerchief discovered any part of her Neck, a Whiteness appeared which the finest *Italian* Paint would be unable to reach. Her Hair was of a Chestnut Brown, and Nature had been extremely lavish to her of it, which she had cut, and on *Sundays* used to curl down her Neck in the modern Fashion. Her Forehead was high, her Eye-brows arched, and rather full than otherwise. Her Eyes black and sparkling; her Nose, just inclining to the *Roman;* her Lips red and moist, and her Under-Lip, according to the Opinion of the Ladies, too pouting. Her Teeth were white, but not exactly even. The Small-Pox had left one only Mark on her Chin, which was so large, it might have been mistaken for a Dimple, had not her left Cheek produced one so near a Neighbour to it, that the former served only for a Foil to the latter. Her Complexion was fair, a little injured by the Sun, but overspread with such a Bloom, that the finest Ladies would have exchanged all their White for it: add to these, a Countenance in which tho' she was extremely bashful, a Sensibility appeared almost incredible; and a Sweetness, whenever she smiled, beyond either Imitation or Description. To conclude all, she had a natural Gentility, superior to the Acquisition of Art, and which surprized all who beheld her. (Bk. 2, ch. 12)

The most substantial difference between this literary portrait and the sketches examined thus far is that this one's primary subject is the physical beauty of the character. It idealizes and elaborates this beauty by enumerating or cataloguing the parts of the body, but most of the portrait is devoted to a minute examination of the face and head. This anatomical catalogue is basic to the structure of many of Fielding's character depictions and varies very little from one idealized figure to another. It usually includes, as in Fanny's case, a description of the hair, forehead, eyebrows, nose, mouth, teeth, lips, complexion, neck, and bosom. Even the order in which these parts are described is fixed; it begins with a brief image of build and proceeds from the head downward. Little attention is paid to clothes, and only the parts of the body normally exposed to sight are mentioned.

Certain standard colors are assigned to the different items of the catalogue. The hair is black or brown, eyebrows are usually black, lips are always red, and teeth are white and even. Complexions are fair, cheeks are a healthy red, and the neck and breasts are white. Certain standard conceits are usually used in the portraits: teeth are compared to ivory, the complexion is a happy combination of lily and rose, the bosom is whiter than lilies, ivory, and alabaster.[19]

This descriptive method is used in the portraits of Fielding's heroes and heroines, as in the depiction of Fanny, Joseph, Tom, and Sophia. Indeed, the techniques of this mode of description—particularly the anatomical catalogue—are used in the presentation of a large number of minor figures throughout the novels. This subject will be treated more fully below, but the task before us at the moment is to determine what traditions Fielding relied on for this device and what his contacts with them were.

The basic characteristics of his idealized descriptions may be found in several places prior to his use of such methods. The two sources of those conventions with which Fielding had most prolonged and intense contact are (1) Greek literature, particularly the love poetry in his Eton textbook, *The Greek Anthology* (in which such conventions were used to present the poet's mistress or a noble lady to the reader), and (2) French and English Renaissance literature, and particularly English Renaissance poetry and French romances, in which these conventions were employed to describe the aristocracy who peopled those genres. While these literatures do not represent Fielding's only contact with these descriptive techniques, there is no evidence to suggest that he had contact with this tradition in such sources as Italian or Provençal poetry, either in the original or in translation. But with regard to these conventions in classical literature the case is very different.

One of the largest collections of love conceits and conventions (almost identical to those in the Renaissance sonnet) is *The Greek Anthology*, a collection of Greek epigrams and other pieces, mostly in elegiac couplets, which date from 700 B.C. to A.D. 1000.[20] A modified version of this convenient anthology, *Poeti Graeci*,[21] containing famous passages from the *Odyssey*, much of Hesiod, Pindar, Theocritus, and Appollonius Rhodius, and the most beautiful of the Greek lyrics, including fragments of Sappho, was one of Fielding's textbooks at Eton.[22] In accord with the normal methods of instruction in classical languages, he was compelled to commit to memory numerous selections from the *Anthology*, after he had studied them minutely, sentence by sentence, line by line.[23] Inter-

estingly enough, the *Anthology* was more than just another school textbook to Fielding; his *Poeti Graeci* was a
part of his library all his life and was sold with the rest of
his books only after his death.[24] Although *The Greek
Anthology* was one of the largest and best-known sources
of literary love conventions, it was not the only such
source available to the author.[25] Therefore, to become
familiar with his knowledge of these conventions, it is
also necessary to refer to similar traditions of description
in other classical and Renaissance writers whose works
Fielding knew.

We will begin with a glance at some of the conceits,
motifs, and methods that Fielding knew from *The Greek
Anthology*, in which the anatomical catalogue is frequently used to depict the poet's love. The following is
the most literal form of this device.

O FEET, O legs, O thighs for which I justly died, O
nates, O pectinem, O flanks, O shoulders, O breasts,
O slender neck, O arms, O eyes I am mad for, O accomplished movement, O admirable kisses, O exclamations that excite.[26]

Such mechanical (and sexist) descriptions are common
in the *Anthology*, and when they are not the principal
focus of the verse they are frequently used as underlying
structural devices.

The passage that follows is a good example of the catalogue functioning as structural technique. Basically a
somewhat impersonal catalogue of beauty, it is not so
unsophisticated and crudely mechanical as the previous
example. In the description of the eyes, hair, and complexion it contains a number of color combinations that
are standard in Fielding's portraits.

> I like them pale, and I also love those with a skin the
> colour of honey, and the fair too; and on the other hand
> I am taken by the black-haired. Nor do I dismiss brown
> eyes; but above all I love sparkling black eyes. (4:285)

The next example contains the conventional colors that
were regularly employed by the Petrarchists, and Fielding, to describe the beloved's mouth and neck.

> Golden are her eyes and her cheeks like crystal, and her
> mouth more delightful than a red rose. Her neck is of
> marble and her bosom polished; her feet are whiter
> than silver Thetis. (1:153)

It is interesting that in this description the idealized beauty
of the girl seems to derive from art rather than nature:
the words "marble" and "polished" liken her features
to those of statuary. From the beginning, indeed, artistic
idealization seems to have involved the collaboration of
all the arts. In the passage quoted above, the loved one is
at last compared to a goddess.

An invocation to the gods and goddesses was another
common method of description in classical literature, as
the following suggests: "Thou hast Hera's eyes, Melite,
and Athene's hands, the breasts of Aphrodite, and the
feet of Thetis" (1:173). This technique of comparing
one aspect of a subject to the same aspect of an idealized,
mythic, and artistic source is also found in Fielding. In the
above example, the lady's breasts are compared to Aphrodite's; and in Fielding's portrait Sophia's bosom is compared to that of the Venus dei Medici. Although this is
the most frequent term of reference in his comparisons,
Fielding's use of this technique was not confined to comparing his characters to works of art (statues, portraits,

paintings); he also compared his very British characters to Greek gods and goddesses. Tom Jones is compared to Adonis, and Susan the chambermaid to Thalestris and her Amazons.

While it seems likely that Fielding's contact with individual techniques of idealized description came from *The Greek Anthology*, its literature did not offer a complete, well-organized model of this descriptive tradition. The closest thing to a model for a full-length, idealized depiction is found not in *The Greek Anthology* but in the dialogues of Lucian. But even though one of Lucian's portraits bears a striking similarity to Fielding's sketches, and therefore merits comparison to his, it seems that the novelist presented his characters only indirectly in the tradition of Lucian. Lucian's portrait describes the mysterious Ionian girl, mistress to an emperor, who is presented in the dialogue between Lycinus and Polystratus titled "A Portrait-Study," which Fielding, with his well-known intimacy with Lucian's writings, must have known.[27] Although there are some important differences between Fielding's and Lucian's descriptions, the latter employed all the basic methods used in *The Greek Anthology* and Fielding's idealized descriptions.

The picture of the Ionian girl is constructed by comparing her physical qualities to the same qualities in the works of various literary and visual Greek artists; and again, poet, painter, and sculptor are collaborators in the production of artistic idealization. The portrait is an anatomical catalogue in which greatest attention is given to the face. And not only is the content of Lucian's catalogue of the face identical to Fielding's but the order is substantially the same (both writers begin with the hair and move downward). The catalogues include, in the same order, the hair, forehead, eyebrows, eyes, and cheeks. Comments on the nose, neck, and lips are also found in both, although in different sequence. Here, then, is the first part of Lucian's description of the Ionian girl:

> She [Reason, who is constructing the portrait] begins with our Cnidian importation, from which she takes only the head; with the rest she is not concerned, as the statue is nude. The hair, the forehead, the exquisite eyebrows, she will keep as Praxiteles has rendered them; the eyes, too, those soft, yet bright-glancing eyes, she leaves unaltered. But the cheeks and the front of the face are taken from the "Garden" Goddess; and so are the lines of the hands, the shapely wrists, the delicately-tapering fingers. Phidias and the Lemnian *Athene* will give the outline of the face, and the well-proportioned nose, and lend new softness to the cheeks; and the same artist may shape her neck and closed lips, to resemble those of his *Amazon.* Calamis adorns her with Sosandra's modesty, Sosandra's grave half-smile; the decent seemly dress is Sosandra's too, save that the head must not be veiled. For her stature, let it be that of Cnidian *Aphrodite;* once more we have recourse to Praxiteles.—What think you, Polystratus? Is it a lovely portrait?[28]

But as Polystratus points out, "colour and tone have a good deal to do with beauty"; so the portrait is given color, and again we encounter the colors which Fielding later employed in his portraits: white, ivory, and rose.

> Euphranor shall colour the hair like his *Hera's;* Polygnotus the comely brow and faintly blushing cheek, after his *Cassandra* in the Assembly-room at Delphi. Polygnotus shall also paint her robe,—of the finest texture, part duly gathered in, but most of it floating in the breeze. For the flesh-tints, which must be neither too

pale nor too high-coloured, Apelles shall copy his own *Campaspe*. And lastly, Aëtion shall give her *Roxana*'s lips. Nay, we can do better: have we not Homer, best of painters, though a Euphranor and an Apelles be present? Let him colour all like the limbs of Menelaus, which he says were "ivory tinged with red." He too shall paint her calm "ox-eyes," and the Theban poet shall help him to give them their "violet" hue. Homer shall add her smile, her white arms, her rosy finger-tips, and so complete the resemblance to golden Aphrodite, to whom he has compared Brises' daughter with far less reason.

In a supplementary description of this beauty's smile, emphasis is placed on the perfect evenness of her teeth, something which Fielding mentions frequently in his idealized descriptions.

But when she smiled, ah! then, Polystratus, I beheld teeth whose whiteness, whose unbroken regularity, who shall describe? Imagine a lovely necklace of gleaming pearls, all of a size; and imagine those dazzling rows set off by ruby lips. In that glimpse, I realized what Homer meant by his "carven ivory." Other women's teeth differ in size; or they project; or there are gaps: here, all was equality and evenness; pearl joined to pearl in unbroken line. Oh, 'twas a wondrous sight, of beauty more than human.

To this portrait of physical beauty Lucian added a description of the girl's mind, claiming (like Fielding) that "where physical perfection goes hand-in-hand with spiritual excellence, there alone (as I maintain) is true beauty."

At the end of this dialogue Lucian, through the mouth of Polystratus, offers an interesting suggestion:

Let us combine our portraits, yours of the body and
mine of the soul, and throw them into a literary form,
for the enjoyment of our generation and of all posterity.
Such a work will be more enduring than those of Apelles and Parrhasius and Polygnotus; it will be far removed from creations of wood and wax and colour,
being inspired by the Muses, in whom alone is that true
portraiture that shows forth in one likeness a lovely
body and a virtuous soul.

Fielding seems to have done this, for when we recall his
statement that he founded his style on Lucian's, and when
we observe the large number of similarities between these
writers, it becomes evident that Fielding's idealized portraits were consciously written in the same tradition as
Lucian's.

Fielding's contact with this tradition in *The Greek
Anthology* and the "Portrait-Study" was reinforced by
what he learned from his textbooks at school. Rhetorical
traditions, from the Middle Ages and earlier, suggest that
a portrait should treat physical and moral traits, but they
do not spell out the method for describing the physical.
However, the examples which rhetoric books regularly
proffered to their readers supplied this omission. Beginning with an apostrophe to nature or God for creating the
subject with such care, the illustrative portraits described
the physiognomy, body, and dress in the same part-by-
part detail and in the same order as the examples in the
Anthology and Lucian's "Portrait-Study."[29] There are,
however, significant differences between these literary
and rhetorical portraits and Fielding's. With the exception of Sophia's portrait, Fielding's are not so loosely
constructed, fragmented, bulky, or extended as Lucian's;
the novelist's physical and mental analyses are packed

into relatively brief descriptions. They have clearly defined boundaries and they are quite close to the independent character sketch in their self-contained form. And instead of being based so completely on explicit comparisons to mythic or artistic models, most of Fielding's portraits merely include references to such figures.

These adaptations of the classical conventions of idealized description were not original in Fielding's work; all may be found in character descriptions in Renaissance literature. The minute similarity between special techniques and content in Renaissance descriptions and in Fielding's idealized presentations forces the conclusion that the novelist's familiarity with this descriptive method also played an important part in shaping his idealized portraiture. The evidence suggests that Renaissance traditions reinforced the methods of the portraits in previous literary and rhetorical works. Beyond that, the more recent modifications of the classical tradition seem to have contributed some of their characteristics to the Renaissance tradition, so that the latter is more than a parallel influence.

The pattern of preferred beauty, which the Renaissance made its own, had its beginnings in classical literature and was presented most prominently in western European literature by Petrarch. It spread rapidly into all the literatures of the Continent and quickly became codified.[30] The English authors who employed this convention and were best known to Fielding include Spenser, Sidney, and Shakespeare. In French literature it was employed by such romance writers as Scudéry, Gomberville, and La Calprenède, whose work Fielding scorned as "those voluminous Works commonly called *Romances*

... which contain, as I apprehend, very little Instruction or Entertainment" (*Joseph Andrews*, preface).

The Renaissance writer approached the problem of portraying human beauty in much the same way as his Greek counterpart.[31] Sight was considered man's noblest sense, and so most description was of physical charm. The human body was "anatomized" and a "beauty of parts" was developed, as the following passage from Scudéry's *Almahide* shows.

> The young *Algadire*, said he, has she nothing in her Eyes that sparkles and pleases? The Complexion of the amiable *Zambrine*, has she nothing that is excellent? The Lily whiteness of the noble *Despine*, does not that dazle thee? *Alicola's* Vermilion, does not that delight thee? The Lips and Teeth of *Miriane*, have they no Charm? The lovely Face of *Meladine*, has that nothing that pleases? The Breasts and plumpness of *Amesabeg*, are not they worth thy taking notice of? The lovely Hands and Arms of the charming *Donique*, will not they move thee? The Shape and Majesty of *Lidice*, do they not attract the Eyes of all the World?[32]

When a lady of outstanding beauty was described, all these parts were combined into a catalogue in which the greatest emphasis was placed on the head and face. The following sonnet by Thomas Watson is a good example and a convenient summary of many of these conventions.

> Her yellowe lockes exceede the beaten goulde;
> Her sparkeling eies in heav'n a place deserve;
> Her forehead high and faire of comely moulde ...
> Each eyebrowe hanges like Iris in the skies;
> Her eagles nose is straight of stately frame;
> On either cheeke a rose and lillie lies ...

Her lips more red than any corall stone;
Her necke more white than aged swans yat mone;
Her breast transparent is like christall rocke;
Her fingers long fit for Apolloes lute.[33]

Again, standard colors were attributed to different parts of the body, and a few of these colors may be detected in the stanza above.

The eyes were generally dark, the eyebrows were black and arched, the cheeks were rosy, the lips were red, the skin was white but frequently tinged with vermilion. Several recurring conceits were employed to describe these colors: the complexion was a mixture of roses and lilies, the lips were coral, the breasts were as white as snow or marble. The following sonnet, by Spenser, also employs most of these colors and conceits.

. . . her ruddy cheekes lyke vnto Roses red:
her snowy browes lyke budded Bellamoures,
her louely eyes lyke Pincks but newly spred.
Her goodly bosome lyke a Strawberry bed,
her neck lyke to a bounch of Cullambynes:
her brest lyke lillyes, ere theyr leaues be shed,
her nipples lyke yong blosomd Iessemynes.[34]

Character presentations in the French romances are even closer in form and content to Fielding's descriptions. These romance portraits adopted the Renaissance type of ideal beauty from the sonneteers and theorists, like Castiglioni and Firenzuola,[35] and around this they developed a rigid formula or mold for describing their people. This formula contains most of the elements we have already seen; however, it casts them in a new form. Portraiture in the romance is an uninterrupted prose description of physical and mental characteristics, complete in itself.

The descriptions begin, as Fielding's do, with an indication of stature. They anatomize the body, emphasizing the face and predicating conventional qualities and colors of the parts they enumerate. The descriptions conclude —again as Fielding's do—with an analysis of the mental characteristics of the individual.

The best way to indicate the similarity between Fielding's descriptions and those in the romances is to set one against the other. Here, for example, is the portrait of Joseph Andrews and that of a nobleman from *Almahide*, Don Alvares, marquess of Monte Major:

Mr. *Joseph Andrews* was now in the one and twentieth Year of his Age. He was of the highest Degree of middle Stature. His Limbs were put together with great Elegance and no less Strength. His Legs and Thighs were formed in the exactest Proportion. His Shoulders were broad and brawny, but yet his Arms hung so easily, that he had all the Symptoms of Strength without the least clumsiness. His Hair was of a nut-brown Colour, and was displayed in wanton Ringlets down his Back. His Forehead was high, his Eyes dark, and as full

He was tall and well limb'd, yet his Demeanour, Gate, and Aspect were altogether so noble, free, and lofty, that they who never saw him before might easily judge him to be a person of an Illustrious descent, His Hair was Chestnut brown, his Cheeks fresh and ruddy, his Eyes black, but little, yet full of Fire and sparkling, his Mouth and Lips rarely proportion'd, & all the Lineaments of his Face very exact. The tone of his voice was lively and somewhat loud. . . . He has a prodigious Wit, courtly, jocund, and indeed the Wit of the of Sweetness as of Fire. His Nose a little inclined to the Roman. His Teeth white and even. His Lips full, red, and soft. His Beard was only rough on his Chin and upper Lip; but his Cheeks, in which his Blood glowed, were overspread with a thick Down. His Countenance had a Tenderness joined with a Sensibility inexpressible. Add to this the most perfect Neatness in his Dress, and an Air, which to those who have not seen many Noblemen, would give an Idea of Nobility. (Bk. 1, ch. 8)

world; so that if I were to draw the Pattern of a true Courtier, that is to say of a person perfectly honest, I verily believe his Portraicture would be a very faithful draught.[36]

One more example should be sufficient to establish Fielding's descriptive tradition—side-by-side portraits of Fielding's Sophia and another aristocrat from *Almahide*, Lydice, "a Person of the highest Quality of any in the Court":

Sophia then, the only daughter of Mr Western, was a middle-sized woman; but rather inclining to tall. Her shape was not only exact, but extremely delicate; and

Her Stature is as goodly as any in the World, and there is something so Noble, so Great, so Majestick in her Port, that you would say she were a Queen. . . . As for the nice proportion of her arms promised the truest symmetry in her limbs. Her hair, which was black, was so luxuriant, that it reached her middle, before she cut it, to comply with the modern fashion; and it was now curled so gracefully in her neck, that few would believe it to be her own. If envy could find any part of her face which demanded less commendation than the rest, it might possibly think her forehead might have been higher without prejudice to her. Her eye-brows were full, even, and arched beyond the power of art to imitate. Her black eyes had a lustre in them, which all her softness could not extinguish. Her nose was exactly regular, and her mouth, in which were two rows of ivory, exactly answered Sir John Suckling's description in those lines.

Her lips were red, and one was thin,

her Hair, Nature had made it of a particular colour, so that you may rather call it *singular*, than *rare*. Her Complexion had all the liveliness, all the whiteness, and all the Carnation of Roses. Her Eyes have had something so sweet, so full of sprightliness, and so piercing, that they gave life to Love, and made the Lover dye. Her Mouth is the Perfection of Natures Workmanship, and the Idea of the most accomplish'd Beauty. For the Oriental Ocean never had Coral or Pearls that might compare with her Lips or Teeth. But Sir, among these Pearls and this Coral there appear'd certain smiles as Charming as the place from whence they sprung. Her Face is Oval, but the proportion thereof so true, and all the Lineaments so admirable, that they were the joy of all Eyes, and the torment of all Hearts. Her Neck is full, and well proportion'd and so

Compar'd to that was
next her chin.
Some bee had stung it
newly.
Her cheeks, were of the
oval kind; and in her
right she had a dimple
which the least smile discovered. Her chin had
certainly its share in
forming the beauty of
her face; but it was dif-
ficult to say it was either
large or small, tho' per-
haps it was rather of the
former kind. Her com-
plexion had rather more
of the lilly than of the
rose; but when exercise,
or modesty, encreased
her natural colour, no
vermilion could equal it.
Then one might indeed
cry out with the cele-
brated Dr Donne.
—Her pure and eloquent
blood
Spoke in her cheeks, and
so distinctly wrought,
That one might almost
say her body thought.
Her neck was long and
finely turned; and here,
if I was not afraid of offending her delicacy, I
might justly say, the

rarely white withal, that
after you have compar'd
it to Snow, Ivory, or
Alabaster, the compari-
sons seem too mean,
since nothing can ap-
proach its Perfection.
As for her Hands and
Arms, they seem'd to be
the height of Nature's
skill, as well for shape as
colour, which are with-
out parallel. In short, it
appears to be infallibly
true, that she has been
altogether Charming, al-
together fair, and that
nothing ever excell'd the
Wonders of her Beauty.
The same thing may be
said of Wit, and the
endowments of her
Mind.[37]

highest beauties of the famous *Venus de Medicis* were outdone. Here was whiteness which no lillies, ivory, nor alabaster could match. The finest cambric might indeed be supposed from envy to cover that bosom, which was much whiter than itself,—it was indeed,

Nitor splendens Pario marmore purius.
'A gloss shining beyond the purest brightness of Parian marble.'

Such was the outside of Sophia; nor was this beautiful frame disgraced by an inhabitant unworthy of it. Her mind was every way equal to her person; nay, the latter borrowed some charms from the former: for when she smiled, the sweetness of her temper diffused that glory over her countenance, which no regularity of features can give. (Bk. 4, ch. 2)

Clearly, Fielding's idealized descriptions belong to a long tradition of portraiture that was used to depict nobility (even royalty) as far back as Greek literature. It is also clear that Fielding's literary portraits belong to the Renaissance branch of that tradition and that his aristocratic audience would have recognized this fact immediately. In a word, Fielding followed a tradition of character description that was well known in his own time and, as we shall see, he did this with specific literary purposes in mind.

Within this genre of description a separate but very important tradition, derived from the visual arts, seems to operate, even in Fielding's idealized descriptions. M. B. Ogle, in attempting to ascertain the origins of this mode of description, suggested that it is doubtless due to the same tendency to elaborate which characterizes Alexandrian art.[38] Is there, in this genre of character portrayal in Alexandrian times and later, an underlying assumption that the arts of painting and sculpturing provide models for the writer in his presentation of the human figure? Ogle implies this, and some of the observations that were made above support his theory. Lucian's references to Praxiteles, Polygnotus, and other contemporary painters and sculptors in his "Portrait-Study" clearly indicate that such an artistic influence is basic to his description of the Ionian girl. Nor is it surprising that Fielding favored this aspect of the descriptive tradition; the practice of describing figures in terms of well-known classical marbles as a means of idealizing them was popular in Fielding's day, as well as in ancient times. It is hardly likely that the novelist missed Pope's use of statuary in his "Temple of Fame," and it is even conceivable that Thomson's use of the *Moral Venus* may have influenced the novelist's use of that statue.[39]

At any rate, the traditions Fielding employed had close ties with the visual arts and external signs of his reliance on them are not difficult to find. In Fanny's portrait he compared the color of her skin to "the finest *Italian Paint*," and other characters are described by reference to Hogarth: Bridget Allworthy, Thwackum, and Deborah Wilkins. A few may even be based on models in Hogarth's plates: Didapper, the city apprentice in *Jonathan Wild*, and Mrs. Tow-wouse.

The portraits themselves are "picturesque": they are capable of being represented in a picture, or they are like a picture.[40] This quality is conveyed by both the organization and the pictorial quality of the individual portraits. The organization is pictorial or, more accurately, portrait-like in that descriptions are set apart from the rest of the novel. They are introduced as rigid set pieces, framed within a formal beginning and a formal end. Inside this framework they first provide a general view of their subject (under the heading "stature") and then develop and expand by means of visual details piled one on top of another. It is in this sense that Fielding's portraits come closest to imitation of the visual arts.

Most of the pictorial qualities, however, are in the details of Fielding's literary portraits. The descriptions are characterized by *stasis*, a distinctive visual quality in which all action stops, and the novelist moves slowly over the fixed features and pose of his subject. Visual detail is emphasized, though this detail is not necessarily empirical, and *enargeia* (used here in the sense of pictorial vividness) is a central value in the portraits.[41] We can "see" Fanny's black, arched eyebrows and the dimple in her cheek. Sophia's luxuriant black hair, which curls down her white neck, is a visual, picturable aspect of her portrait. This type of visual detail (and others of a pictorial nature) plays an important part in the success of Fielding's character presentations and it would be wrong to disregard them or to miss their significance.

IV

The final method of Fielding's characterization is so closely related to his idealized portraiture as to be a variation of it, although he used it exclusively to portray villains and rogues. One of the best examples of it is his portrait of the effete beau Didapper.

> Mr. *Didapper*, or Beau *Didapper*, was a young Gentleman of about four Foot five Inches in height. He wore his own Hair, tho' the Scarcity of it might have given him sufficient Excuse for a Periwig. His Face was thin and pale: The Shape of his Body and Legs none of the best; for he had very narrow Shoulders, and no Calf; and his Gait might more properly be called hopping than walking. The Qualifications of his Mind were well adapted to his Person. We shall handle them first negatively. He was not entirely ignorant: For he could talk a little *French*, and sing two or three *Italian* Songs: He had lived too much in the World to be bashful, and too much at Court to be proud: He seemed not much inclined to Avarice; for he was profuse in his Expenses: Nor had he all the Features of Prodigality; for he never gave a Shilling:—No Hater of Women; for he always dangled after them; yet so little subject to Lust, that he had, among those who knew him best, the Character of great Moderation in his Pleasures. No Drinker of Wine; nor so addicted to Passion, but that a hot Word or two from an Adversary made him immediately cool. (Bk. 4, ch. 9)

This picture is constructed on much the same plan as the portraits of Joseph and Tom, and it follows the formula we observed in the works of Scudéry and the Renaissance writers. The portrait begins with a mention of stature and is "fleshed out" by the standard anatomical catalogue. The same descending order observed in the idealized descriptions is employed in this portrait, and little attention is paid to clothes. On the other hand, this descriptive method is less full, more economical, and less painfully detailed than the portraiture just examined. The principal difference, however, between idealized description and this method, which we will call portrait caricature, is in the contents of the anatomical catalogue. Like its Italian predecessor, Fielding's caricature is a reversal or countertendency to his ideal portraits.

What Hagstrum says of caricature in Augustan poetry accurately describes what Fielding is doing here: "The art of distortion is to the art of idealization what bathos is to hypsos—an exact inversion, to which the same techniques apply, though the direction is down and not up. The art of distorting reality is the precise reversal of *la belle nature*. It is nature consummately wrought down to a lower pitch."[42]

In place, then, of the warm, nearly sentimental, generalized beauty of the idealized portraits we find a Hogarthian quality in Fielding's caricature. The term "Hogarthian" seems appropriate, not merely because the novelist's description is graphic and visually vivid but also because Fielding certainly received an impetus from Hogarth in the pictorial representation of his "low" characters.[43] This will become evident when we treat the individual portraits.

This descriptive method creates a vivid picture of an ugly character from accurately observed details, which usually represent a deformity of several or all of the physical features in the anatomical catalogue. Human parts are altered beyond recognizable shape, twisted into freakish order, or omitted entirely. From these details a portrait of extraordinary ugliness results which represents, by its particularity—by its eccentricity and aggregate of deformity—a brilliant contrast to the generalized and rather celestial beauty of the heroes and heroines.

Despite Fielding's disavowal of caricature in the preface to *Joseph Andrews* the term "portrait caricature" can be used to describe some of the novelist's depictions.[44] Clearly, he exaggerates and debases details of physical appearance for satiric purposes and renders his figures ridiculous without entirely destroying their natural appearance. He distorts, but does not destroy, the normal human outlines of his subjects; we never forget that the figure is a human being. Slipslop's eyes are too small and her nose is too large; Tow-wouse has a strange projection in the middle of her forehead, a projection which somehow becomes her nose. Still, both are credible as persons despite their deformity.

Just as Fielding's idealized portraiture reflects his approval of the figures so described, his portrait caricature is a reflection or an emblem of his attitude toward his rogues and villains. Although the people he caricatures might appear to be no more than exuberantly comic characters, this is not the case. Each figure is founded on a moral quality or trait (usually a vice or affectation) that Fielding fears and hates: hypocrisy, pride, lust, avarice. The trait may be suppressed by a humorous appearance, but it is not eliminated. All the people he caricatures are morally and psychologically rogues; each, in his own way, is the reverse of what Fielding holds up as an ideal in his novels.

One important aspect of caricature may seem to be

missing from Fielding's portraits: the opportunity to
compare the caricature with the original, so that we can
appreciate what Gombrich and Kris called "the witty
play of 'like in unlike.' "[45] While the original is literally
missing, there is still a point of reference or comparison
for these caricatures, and so this "witty play" exists in the
novels. The point of comparison is the idealized description, whose perfection is the norm or touchstone against
which the ugliness of the caricatures is to be judged. The
particularity of the latter inevitably exposes them as
divergent from the ideal portraits, which are granted a
measure of universality in that they are not recognizable
as distinct individuals. The caricatures must have appeared as "originals" to Fielding's contemporaries and
would have been quickly recognized and condemned by
the eighteenth-century reader.[46] In this way the different
classes of characters interact to define each other's function and meaning within the novels.

While some of Fielding's caricature consists merely in
the distortion of human features for the visually repelling
effects just described, much of it is richer and more subtle
in its design than straightforward, literal portraiture. Most
often he manipulates and exploits the natural details of
appearance to give an allegorical or emblematic dimension to his characters, and he does this by drawing on the
riches of both the visual and literary traditions of the
period. In the seventeenth and the eighteenth century,
moral and intellectual abstractions were frequently visual-
ized as icons and emblems. In Cesare Ripa's *Moral Emblems* (1709), a storehouse of such devices, vices, virtues,
and psychological qualities appear as human figures,
prominently accompanied by animals that are symbolic
of the appropriate abstractions. In mythology and litera-

ture, and folklore as well, a number of abstract traits were identified with animals that were believed to embody those human qualities. Such identifications come from sources as different as Greek and Roman myths and medieval bestiaries.

Fielding relies on these and similar traditions to give his characters emblematic and allegorical natures. Choosing animals that are symbolic of the moral or intellectual qualities he sees in a figure, he used them as a subtle, organizing principle in his portrait caricatures. Molding the face and body of a personage to fit the characteristic features of the animal he has chosen, Fielding identifies his figure with an established literary or visual emblem. Behind Slipslop's face the reader sees the head of a cow. Mrs. Tow-wouse's face and body are formed in the image of a stoat or weasel. Using graphic, natural detail, the novelist rendered his abstractions, personifications, and allegorical qualities in a concrete, sensuous manner. Without destroying the authenticity of a figure's looks, he molded normal features so that they could carry emblematic weight while remaining both natural and comic.

These are the principal traditions from which Fielding drew his portraiture. The substance of this study is devoted to showing how the novelist used these modes of depiction to construct and enrich his character drawing. The study identifies the emblematic, idealized, or allegorical qualities of the figures in each novel and establishes their nature. It looks at Fielding's variations of, and gradual departures from, the major prototypes outlined above. It relates his portraiture to the themes and purposes within each work, and it attempts to throw light on the general nature of his characterization and its development in the course of his career as a novelist.

CHAPTER TWO

Jonathan Wild

NLIKE FIELDING'S other prose fiction, *Jonathan Wild* is organized in a manner that makes it difficult to classify. Overtly political at points and intensely ethical throughout, the tale of Wild's life is closer in form to *Rasselas* and *Candide* than to *Joseph Andrews* or *Tom Jones*. Suggesting an affinity to the sermon or homily, Fielding called it a "history, which will, we hope, produce much better lessons, and more instructive, than any we can preach."

The most accurate analysis of its form describes it as an apologue, a fictional example of the truth of a set of formulable statements.[1] The justness of this description is immediately apparent in the preface to *Jonathan Wild*, where Fielding closely formulates the statements that suggest the structure and purpose of the work. The subject of the book, he says, is the distinction between "greatness" (which, like the term "great man," he uses ironically) and its antithesis, goodness.

> The Truth, I apprehend, is, we often confound the Ideas of Goodness and Greatness together, or rather include the former in our Idea of the latter. If this be so, it is surely a great Error, and no less than a Mistake of

the Capacity for the Will. In Reality, no Qualities can be more distinct: for as it cannot be doubted but that Benevolence, Honour, Honesty, and Charity, make a good Man; and that Parts, Courage, are the efficient Qualities of a Great Man, so must it be confess'd, that the Ingredients which compose the former of these Characters, bear no Analogy to, nor Dependence on those which constitute the latter. A Man may therefore be Great without being Good, or Good without being Great.[2]

Defining his theme and purpose, he also says:

This Bombast Greatness then is the Character I intend to expose; and the more this prevails in and deceives the World, taking to itself not only Riches and Power, but often Honour, or at least the Shadow of it, the more necessary it is to strip the Monster of these false Colours, and shew it in its native Deformity: for by suffering Vice to possess the Reward of Virtue, we do a double Injury to Society, by encouraging the former, and taking away the chief Incentive to the latter. (Preface, p. xxx)

How does this particular purpose and the literary form it takes affect character drawing? What kinds of characters are found in an apologue, and what techniques are used to present them? How are they related to one another? Are characters in an apologue more allegorical than those in Fielding's novels or, as some have held, are they "flesh and blood" in a similar manner?

I

One of the first things the reader is likely to notice about the characters in *Jonathan Wild* is that they are arranged along highly rhetorical lines. Rhetorical theory declares that every question necessarily has at least two sides to it. The ability to see both sides of a question is central to the formulation of conflicts of character and theme in literature,[3] and this rhetorical approach is a very basic organizing principle in this biography. On its most obvious level, two archetypal characters are portrayed: the villain is introduced as "Mr. Jonathan Wild the Great" and Heartfree, Wild's moral opposite in every imaginable sense, is defined (later in the book, in response to Wild) as of "a stamp entirely different from what we have hitherto dealt in." The "good natured" Heartfree and the "great" Wild represent not only two contrasting touchstones in their respective qualities but the antithetic poles around which, without a single important exception, the other significant characters gravitate. For each character on one side of a question there is usually a character on the other who is the former's moral antithesis. However, for the sake of maintaining the appearances of biography, which is crucial to the political message, the symmetrical arrangement is not carried to its extreme conclusion.

Wild's character receives more formal attention than any other figure in the novel. In a real sense, the book is a long, biographical character sketch of the protagonist. There are two important sections in *Jonathan Wild* in which the "great man" (the term is used ironically throughout) is characterized directly: its opening, which is a formulary biography, and its conclusion, which is a full chapter of psychological and dramatic characterization. When the titles of the first section, the beginning chapters, are juxtaposed with the schematization of the oration for praise from Rainolde's *Foundacion of Rhe-*

torike,[4] the pattern for the initial characterization and for the work itself becomes clear.[5]

Jonathan Wild	"Oration of Praise or Blame"
Chapter I. Showing the wholesome uses drawn from recording the achievements of those wonderful productions of nature called GREAT MEN.	The order to make this Oracion is thus declared.
Chapter II. Giving an account of as many of our hero's ancestors as can be gathered out of the rubbish of antiquity. . .	Firste, for the enteryng of the matter, you shall place a exordium, or beginnyng.
Chapter III. The birth, parentage, and education of Mr. Jonathan Wild the Great.	The seconde place, you shall bryng to his praise, Genus eius, that is to saie: Of what kinde he came of, whiche dooeth consiste in fower pointes. Of what nacion. Of what countree. Of what auncetours. Of what parentes.
	After that you shall declare, his educacion. . . .
	Then put there to that, whiche is the chief grounde of al praise: his actes doen. . . .

The material in the chapters reflects this rhetorical pattern even better than the chapter titles. Every major category that is outlined in the scheme is included in the work; even the order of these *topoi* is preserved. And with very good reason. The use of this well-known rhetorical pattern is of great value to the narrator at this introductory point. The formula is ideally suited to presenting a generalized figure, like Wild, whom Fielding intends as a type of the great man. But beyond that it is rich in associations that are useful to the writer's satiric purposes.

The primary function of this device is service in an oration of praise, as Rainolde's *Rhetorike* indicates, but it also recommends these same categories for blame. Relying on his educated reader's knowledge of the ambiguous or reversible uses of this rhetorical device, Fielding ostensibly employs the *topoi* or places for praise, as one would expect them to be used in characterizing the hero of a biography. However, he fills the *topoi* with matter for blame, or matter which is "low." In this way the formula performs both of its antithetic purposes at once. It permits the writer to maintain the appearance of a traditional laudatory biography while enabling him to carry out his satiric intent. So the ironic history properly incorporates an ironic panegyric in which the narrator blames, while seeming to praise, Wild and his kind.

These *topoi* had other associations as well. They were used by classical writers to structure their biographies of heroes and great men, and later were employed by Fielding's contemporaries in their lives of English saints and noblemen. In portraying Jonathan Wild the writer was careful to invoke these elevated associations: he makes extended, specific use of the *topoi* in the form in which they were employed by hagiographers and biographers, and he mentions Plutarch, Nepos, and Suetonius by name. Having thus established the dignified association of these places, he applies them to the life of a crook. In this context they become perfect devices for implementing the mock-heroic intent of this biography. The dignified formula is used to generate and organize material that concerns a petty thief, and thereby stresses the criminality and meanness of the "great" Wild. These sublime *topoi*, previously used to describe the lives of Caesar and Alexander (famous if not moral men), are filled by trivia, absurd apocrypha, superstition, and even gossip.

The artificially elaborate accounts of petty thievery undercut the classical splendor of the *topoi*, and the *topoi*, in turn, emphasize the insignificant nature of the biographical matter. This incongruity generates a contrast between the high vehicle and the low tenor that is, first of all, an ironic comment on Wild and, secondly, a pointed attack on the traditional elevation of military and political figures to the rank of heroes or great men. As William J. Farrell writes, "The bombast structure implies, indeed underlines the bombast greatness of not only Wild but others who, though conventionally presented in this form, are as unworthy of it as he is."[6]

In addition to its broad mock-heroic purpose, this sketch makes a number of satiric points. At several places the topics of the biography present an ironic and pointed parallel to the education and training of the average eighteenth-century nobleman; a prison term in America, for example, is equated with the grand tour, which was part of every nobleman's training.[7] Noblemen in general, however, are not Fielding's only target. His account of Wild's ancestry is the first indication that the living inspiration of the biography was Robert Walpole. Walpole's grandfather was named Edward, the name accorded so prominently to a significant number of Wild's ancestors; and—to the amusement of his enemies—the prime minister's much satirized lineage had been the subject of a book (just prior to the publication of *Jonathan Wild*) titled the *Brief and True History of Robert Walpole and his Family From Their Original to the Present Time* by William Musgrave.[8]

In the initial chapter the direct analysis of character is limited to a brief sentence of psychological characterization, before the biographical sketch. This ironic passage establishes the necessary identification between Wild and the abstraction he personifies. "As our hero had as little as perhaps is to be found of that meanness [goodness], indeed only enough to make him partaker of the imperfection of humanity . . . we have ventured to call him *The Great;* nor do we doubt but our reader, when he hath perused his story, will concur with us in allowing him that title" (bk. 1, ch. 1). Following this offhand, conversational piece, the introductory characterization turns into an ironic narrative of objective biographical events, chosen and organized to illustrate the moral composition of Wild's character. These events shade into the action of the novel when the formula is abandoned in chapter 4.

The climactic depiction of Jonathan Wild occurs in the final chapter of the book, under the title "The character of our hero, and the conclusion of this history." This portrait is both an organic part of the apologue and a sketch apart, sufficient unto itself. First of all, it is a "bringing together [of] those several features as it were of his mind which lie scattered up and down in this history, to present our readers with a perfect picture of greatness." It is a summary and final evaluation of Wild's actions and nature throughout the book, but it is also "a perfect picture of greatness," an abstract and highly stereotyped sketch of that ethical figure, the great man. Through Wild we see Caesar, Alexander, Walpole, and beyond these individuals we see the historical type that includes all great men.

This final portrait of the great man is presented primarily in the form of an English character sketch, which takes the concept of greatness and defines it as a complex of psychological and moral qualities. The sketch opens with a psychological analysis of a great man, which derives from the ethical theorizing in the book's preface.

> As his most powerful and predominant passion was ambition, so nature had, with consummate propriety, adapted all his faculties to the attaining [of] those glorious ends to which this passion directed him. He was extremely ingenious in inventing designs, artful in contriving the means to accomplish his purposes, and resolute in executing them; for as the most exquisite cunning and most undaunted boldness qualified him for any undertaking, so was he not restrained by any of those weaknesses which disappoint the views of mean and vulgar souls. (Bk. 4, ch. 15)

Because of its laudatory rhetoric and ironic tone, this sketch seems to present a rather normal if aggressive type. The qualities chosen to denominate the great man are not dangerous *per se*, Fielding seems to say, but are amoral, ambiguous characteristics.

It is only in the elaborate denigration of honesty that follows that the reader is given a negative context for the ethos just described. Wild is not restrained by any of those qualities

> which are comprehended in one general term of honesty, which is a corruption of HONOSTY, a word derived from what the Greeks call an ass. He was entirely free from those low vices of modesty and good nature, which, as he said, implied a total negation of human greatness, and were the only qualities which absolutely rendered a man incapable of making a considerable figure in the world. (Ibid.)

The previous analysis attributed mental qualities to Wild, and this one, playful and ironic, denies him those of the heart. A great man, in Fielding's mind, has strong, intellectualized, aggressive tendencies but no positive moral values to guide them. The two key *lacunae* are modesty and good nature. The lack of the first gives free reign to pride and egotism and the absence of benevolence, the cardinal virtue in all Fielding's heroes and heroines, removes any concern for mankind.

Fielding began by describing Jonathan Wild in terms of psychological qualities; he then proceeded to characterize him in terms of the virtues he does not possess. Now, in a passage quite changed in tone, he describes him in terms of his vices.

> His lust was inferior only to his ambition; but, as for what simple people call love, he knew not what it was. His avarice was immense, but it was of the rapacious, not of the tenacious kind; his rapaciousness was indeed so violent, that nothing ever contented him but the whole; for, however considerable the share was which his coadjutors allowed him of a booty, he was restless in inventing means to make himself master of the smallest pittance reserved by them. (Ibid.)

In this apt, pithy summary of Wild's life, Fielding is unwilling to sustain his irony; his manner is detached and factual and his sentiments are direct. Indeed, rather than suggesting a character analysis, this passage resembles a condemnation and exposure of Wild, containing, in its mention of lust and avarice, a final moral judgment of the great man's nature.

The next part of the sketch (constituting the bulk of the chapter) moves from summary to dramatic characterization as Fielding illustrates the previous analysis by describing some typical manifestations of certain traits in the speech, thought, and writings of the great man. The stereotype's avarice, rapaciousness, and cunning are again emphasized. The great man's most esteemed vice, however, is hypocrisy, a vice that seems to have obsessed Fielding and one he often mentions in his description of Wild's physiognomy. "The character which he most valued himself upon, and which he principally honored in others, was that of hypocrisy." Fifteen "maxims as the certain methods of attaining greatness," devised by Wild, are also quoted in this sketch. These contain little that is new; repetitious statements, they are representative of the great man's character as it has just been described.

At this point the character sketch draws to an end and Wild's name (absent since the first line of the portrait to emphasize the generic nature of the sketch and permit the reader to apply the character to Walpole and his kind) is again introduced, as the author points to the perfect alignment between the hero and his principles. He is compared again with Alexander and Caesar, and the sketch concludes:

> Now, in Wild everything was truly great, almost without alloy, as his imperfections (for surely some small ones he had) were only such as served to denominate him a human creature, of which kind none ever arrived great rogue are synonymous terms, so long shall Wild at consummate excellence. . . . Indeed, while greatness consists in power, pride, insolence, and doing mischief to mankind—to speak out—while a great man and a stand unrivaled on the pinnacle of GREATNESS. (Ibid.)

Beginning in his usual, even tone, the narrator gradually abandons it, and in the last sentence openly equates the great man and the rogue; and more intensely and forthrightly than before, the history's ironic pretense of praising Wild and his kind is suspended. But as one form of irony falls away (ironic statement), the history ends on another, more jarring form—an irony based on the incongruities in political and economic reality: "A great man and a great rogue are synonymous terms."

If Wild is the most eminent example of "greatness" in the history, he is not the only one. He is surrounded by a large contingent that shares his characteristics, two or three of whom seem to have been created by the narrator as foils to Wild's and each other's greatness. Clearly, Marybone and Fireblood, introduced together, are intended to establish such a contrast between themselves and to constitute, with Wild, a spectrum or panorama of greatness that is to refine the reader's awareness of the nature and composition of this quality. The first of these is Mr. Marybone, a minor figure who is not formally characterized beyond the fact that his name, with appropriate foreboding, seems to signify Tyburn.[9] Introduced to show that it is possible to be a common criminal without being, in any true sense, a great man (his character is established by the fact that he will rob but not murder), he makes his entrance and exit in a single chapter. This fleeting appearance suggests that he functions only as a negative example of greatness and as a foil to Fireblood, another gang member who appears on the scene immediately after Marybone's execution.

Fireblood, who represents a kind of self-interest much closer to Wild's and a special if diminished kind of greatness, is presented with considerable care and detail.

The name of this youth, who will hereafter make some figure in this history, being the Achates of our Aeneas, or rather the Haephestion of our Alexander, was Fireblood. He has every qualification to make a second-rate GREAT man; or, in other words, he was completely equipped for the tool of a real or first-rate GREAT man. We shall therefore (which is the properest way of dealing with this kind of GREATNESS) describe him negatively, and content ourselves with telling our reader what qualities he had not; in which number were humanity, modesty, and fear, not one grain of any of which was mingled in his whole composition. (Bk. 3, ch. 4)

This brief, psychological character is among Fielding's most economical, direct, and pointed sketches. The comparison of Fireblood to Achates and Wild to Aeneas re-creates much of the same mock-heroic effect produced at the introduction of Wild himself; again, the obvious differences between the great man and the man of epic stature are called to mind. Moreover, there is an added irony in this comparison because Achates is a synonym for a close and faithful friend, and the mutually exploitative relationship between Wild and Fireblood is, of course, a parody of such comradeship.

The second comparison (of Fireblood to Haephestion and Wild to Alexander) invokes the rather subtle but fundamental similarities between criminals and politicians. This is especially true of the effects of this comparison since, by mentioning Alexander the Great, Fielding associates all his great men with an imperialist general whom many eighteenth-century readers considered an infamous villain.[10] In identifying Wild and his men with such a person, here and throughout the work, Fielding keeps a relevant, well-known example of the type before the reader which, without destroying the ironic tone of the characterization, points to the historic reality that great men represent.

The final part of Fireblood's character sketch is a simple, generic picture of a second-rate great man. The picture is composed of half of Wild's qualities—his negative ones. The hero of the biography is described as lacking in honesty, modesty, and good nature; Fireblood is without fear, modesty, and humanity. He is just as amoral as Wild but not so ambitious. Appropriately enough, it is this gang member, with qualities close to his own, who causes Wild's undoing.

A third kind of greatness, somewhere between Mary-bone's and Fireblood's, is represented by another member of Wild's gang, Blueskin.

> There was in the gang a man named Blueskin, one of those merchants who trade in dead oxen, sheep, &c., in short, what the vulgar call a butcher. This gentleman had two qualities of a great man, viz.: undaunted courage, and an absolute contempt of those ridiculous distinctions of *meum* and *tuum*, which would cause endless disputes, did not the law happily decide them by converting both into *suum*. The common form of exchanging property by trade seemed to him too tedious; he therefore resolved to quit the mercantile profession, and, falling acquainted with some of Mr. Wild's people, he provided himself with arms, and enlisted of the gang; in which he behaved for some time with great decency and order, and submitted to accept such share of the booty with the rest as our hero allotted him.
>
> But this subserviency agreed ill with his temper; for we should have before remembered a third heroic qual-

ity, namely, ambition, which was no inconsiderable part of his composition. (Bk. 3, ch. 14)

The sketch opens on a mock-epic note: Blueskin's common or "low" occupation is described in an elevated style, and then revealed with startling bluntness. The man begins as a butcher and he remains one—he deals with people instead of oxen when he joins Wild. In many ways this sketch is typical of the character drawing in *Jonathan Wild*. Ironic in manner and aimed at depicting a simple, ethical personage, it describes Blueskin in terms of a few broad qualities that place him in the moral scheme of the book. With three positive qualities of the original great man and no negative ones, he takes his place between Marybone and Fireblood in the chain of greatness. To this direct psychological characterization the writer adds, in comic, elevated language, a short biographical narrative. Blueskin's entry into Wild's gang, formulated as a reasoned, logical progress and expressed in formal, syllogistic rhetoric, matches the author's parody of the butcher's oversophisticated cogitations on the conventions of private property expressed in the unlikely form of Latin pronouns.

II

The Heartfrees are introduced in the beginning of book 2. Reflecting on the processes of his art (the passage is similar to but less elaborate than the later novel's preliminary chapters), the narrator says:

One reason why we chose to end our first book, as we did, with the last chapter, was, that we are now obliged to produce two characters of a stamp entirely different from what we have hitherto dealt in. These persons are of that pitiful order of mortals who are in contempt called good-natured. (Bk. 2, ch. 1)

This significant introduction, as we suggested earlier, indicates the role of the Heartfrees in the book. Linked closely to Wild, the writer creates them in a manner which suggests the destructive bond he believes exists between the good and the great. Significantly, no initial distinction is made between the individual Heartfrees, or indeed among good-natured people in general. Both are described as belonging to a certain "order of mortals" or class and their common personality is established with a directness and simplicity appropriate to their functional nature.

After the common introduction, the narrator first treats of Thomas Heartfree's character. In contrast to the grand manner at Wild's debut, the style is direct and unaffected but for an occasional transparently ironic remark. The writer introduces Heartfree by means of a brief biography which emphasizes his similarity to the great man in matters of age, education, and background—setting the hero and villain up as products of similar environments in much the same way as he would later do with Tom Jones and Blifil. Again stressing the comparative function of Heartfree in the history, Fielding analyzes his nature. "As our reader is to be more acquainted with this person, it may not be improper to open somewhat his character, especially as it will serve as a kind of foil to the noble and great disposition of our hero."

The character sketch begins with the mention of his name, which points to Heartfree's most basic and consuming virtue, his naturally good heart. The rest of the characterization defines and illustrates what is implied in his name. Heartfree is "of an honest and open disposition," the narrator tells us, which is confirmed by the biographical information about his beliefs. He belongs to "that sort of men whom experience only, and not their own natures, must inform that there are such things as deceit and hypocrisy in the world." The core of his character is composed of "several great weaknesses of mind, being good-natured, friendly, and generous to a great excess." The sketch concludes with three typical manifestations of these virtues in the business and domestic life of Heartfree. At this point the work moves into a rather polemical description of Mrs. Heartfree.

In the analysis of Heartfree the narrator is concerned with a limited number of moral and psychological qualities which he judges to be involved in a discussion of greatness and goodness and which consequently recur in the description of all the main figures. As we might expect, the qualities of Heartfree's ethos are sentimental virtues and are directly and rather simply related to or contrasted with those of Wild. The first quality mentioned by the narrator is Heartfree's honesty, whereas Wild is said to have none of the weaknesses which "are comprehended in one general term of honesty . . . a word derived from what the Greeks call an ass." Heartfree has an open, unhypocritical disposition; Wild holds that "the heart was the proper seat of hatred, and the countenance of affection and friendship" (bk. 4, ch. 15). The jeweller is "generous," the great man is "avaricious"; the former is "good-natured," the latter is "free from those low vices of modesty and of good-nature." Heartfree is "friendly," Wild is "rapacious." No aspect of the parallel between these two men is omitted; it is worked out on a point-for-point, almost programmatic comparison in which the focus is on the basic qualities which divide these men: rapacious ambition and middle-class moral benevolence.

This portrait of Heartfree is an ironic description of a type common in Fielding's work, the benevolent man. The sketch, brief as it is, presents the full outline of the type. And although it is an economical and exact analysis, there is not the same energy or interest in probing the nature of goodness in the Job-like Heartfree as in analyzing Wild's greatness. Wild is much more complex, more difficult to encompass—larger, more powerful, more fascinating; as an intellectual image of the "deformity of vice," he is a persuasive figure. Heartfree's character can never escape its fate—its *raison d'être* is Wild. Locked in uneven contrast with the protagonist, Heartfree emerges merely as a flat, passive "answer" to Jonathan Wild. His character fails to convince not because he is a flat character (almost all the figures in the book are) but because he does not vitally and credibly represent the side of the novel's central dichotomy that he embodies.

Like Wild, Heartfree has his followers. The most obvious of these is his apprentice, Friendly, who as a sort of second-rate benevolent man is intended as a support for Heartfree and a contrast to Fireblood. Friendly's character is not sketched; his simple nature needs no elaboration (Fielding's good figures are generally much less complicated than his villains). Called "the good apprentice," Jack Friendly's name and the uncommon height of friendship he shows his master are sufficient to explain him.

Heartfree's second follower, his wife, is characterized in a few lines at the end of her husband's sketch. She is a woman who, with an agreeable person, was a mean-spirited, poor, domestic, low-bred animal, who confined herself mostly to the care of her family, placed her happiness in her husband and her children, followed no expensive fashions or diversions, and indeed rarely went abroad, unless to return the visits of a few plain neighbors, and twice a year afforded herself, in company with her husband, the diversion of a play, where she never sat in a higher place than the pit. (Bk. 2, ch. 1)

The unwittingly grim picture presented in this analysis and its illustration is that of a faceless, supportive wife who has no real existence apart from her husband, her children, and her dreary household duties. This judgment is adequate to the unsubstantial Mrs. Heartfree before she is kidnaped by Wild, but it bears only the most tenuous relationship to the self-confident, commanding, even vain woman who tells of her very undomestic adventures (most of them sexual) in a manner so absorbed and self-conscious as to indicate her own involvement and admiration of them. As a result of her central role in the elaborate and fantastic romance that concludes the book, she develops into a complex figure; and what was conceived as a comprehensively descriptive character sketch ultimately turns out to be an unconscious parody of what Mrs. Heartfree is at the end. Consequently, she is the most involved figure in the book and, as a developing character among types, the one least at home in her setting.

Not all the figures in *Jonathan Wild* are presented by psychological and dramatic characterization. For most of the descriptions, admittedly, the author employs the direct style, recommended in Lucian's *Quomodo Historia Scribenda Sit* (and overwhelmingly employed in works like Fielding's in the eighteenth century),[11] yet a few figures are depicted at considerable length by a full, elaborate description of appearance, clothes, and the like. Tishy, Smirk, and Bagshot are described by this method, and their portraits are the "poetical embellishments" and "descriptions" which Fielding took "every occasion of interspersing" (*Tom Jones*, bk. 4, ch. 1) in his narrative to liven and amplify it. This group of characters is not presented only in terms of physical detail, however. As we have suggested, they possess qualities that make them part of the general moral scheme of the history and part of a smaller pattern, which centers on Tishy.

Tishy is the person in this group who receives the most elaborate characterization. She is first described as her lover, or rather suitor, sees her on a purposeful morning visit.

Her lovely hair hung wantonly over her forehead, being neither white with, nor yet free from, powder; a neat double clout, which seemed to have been worn a few weeks only, was pinned under her chin; some remains of that art with which ladies improve nature shone on her checks; her body was loosely attired, without stays or jumps, so that her breasts had uncontrolled liberty to display their beauteous orbs, which they did as low as her girdle; a thin covering of a rumpled muslin handkerchief almost hid them from the eyes, save in a few parts, where a good-natured hole gave opportunity to the naked breast to appear. Her gown was a satin of a whitish color, with about a dozen little silver spots upon it, so artificially interwoven at great distance, that they looked as if they had fallen there by chance. This, flying open, discovered a fine yellow petticoat, beautifully edged round the bottom with a narrow piece of half gold lace, which was now almost become fringe; beneath this appeared another petticoat stiffened with

whalebone, vulgarly called a hoop, which hung six
inches at least below the other; and under this again
appeared an undergarment of that color which Ovid
intends when he says,
　—Qui color albus erat nunc est contrarius albo.
She likewise displayed two pretty feet covered with
silk and adorned with lace, and tied, the right with a
handsome piece of blue ribbon; and the left, as more
unworthy, with a piece of yellow stuff, which seemed
to have been a strip of her upper petticoat. Such was the
lovely creature whom Mr. Wild attended. (Bk. 1, ch. 9)

This is indeed a skillful portrait. Introduced not at
Tishy's first appearance in the history but at Wild's first
sexual encounter with the lady, it describes her as the
excited gentleman would have seen her. By its preoccupation with the externals of dress and figure (it glances over
her countenance and concentrates on her seminude
figure), it emphasizes her status as the object of Wild's
lust. Thus it forms a realistic background for his attempted rape, and at the same time tells us about her
nature. Organized in a painterly manner, the picture is
set in a verbal frame that begins with a description of her
soiled hair and moves downward to detail her painted
cheeks, her partially exposed body, her clothes, and
finally, her silk-covered feet, one of which is tied with a
blue ribbon (symbolic of the Order of the Garter).[12]
The portrait ends with a summarizing line that constitutes
its outer boundary or frame.
　Within the pictorially ordered framework a number of
other visual techniques are employed to describe Tishy.
Most of her appearance—her dress, for little else about her
is noticed—is described in *stasis* and is portrayed in an empirical manner (unusual with Fielding) that depends for

its effect on detail and color. However, to counter the static quality achieved by these methods, to impart liveliness to the figure, and to sustain the sense of narrative, "motion" (largely sexual interest) is introduced into the scene: Tishy's breasts "display their beauteous orbs" and her petticoat flies open.

The form of the portrait, with its well-defined beginning and end, indicates that it is based on the traditional Renaissance literary portrait. The detailed depiction of Tishy's clothing, though at once grand and tawdry, suggests that it was modeled on the literary portraits of royal figures whose dress was elaborately described in contemporary romances. Tishy's delineation, then, is a mock-heroic portrait of a royal or courtly figure—a situation that generates a number of comic ironies. The dignity and grace associated with the normal uses of this form of portraiture are travestied by its debasement, in which the form for picturing royalty is employed to portray a mercenary and unprincipled charlatan. There is even the suggestion that the writer is burlesquing these portraits and their originals, particularly in the despised romance, by the fact that he follows the form so closely.

But clothing is not the only interesting texture in this description. In other important details this verbal picture is remarkably similar to the traditional royal portrait, with its rosy cheeked, long-haired, full-figured woman. The difference is that this glorious picture is undermined by small but subversive modifications. In contrast to someone like Fanny, who is a paragon of nature, Tishy's appearance is based on the spurious values of art. Her hair is "neither white with, nor yet free from, powder," her clout is unlaundered; her cheeks, instead of having a natural rosy color, are artificially but tellingly painted. Her body is "loosely attired" in both a physical and symbolic sense. Her handkerchief is rumpled and has a "good-natured hole," from which her breast artfully appears. And her white petticoat is dirty, although the writer points this out with assumed dignity and indirection, in ironic deference to the "grandeur" of his subject, by quoting Ovid to that effect. By means of these details there emerges from this formally dignified description of a vivid portrait of a sluttish girl who is posing as a woman of status and quality. The incongruity between form and matter, between appearance and reality, between pretense and actuality makes this the most striking portrait in the history.

Tishy Snap is the female counterpart of the great man and her antithesis is clearly Mrs. Heartfree, who is the personification of feminine modesty and wifely virtue. Tishy's predominant passions are vanity, lust, and avarice. To attend to these needs she chooses three great men, each with a single but appropriate dimension of greatness. "To satisfy the first of these she employed Mr. Smirk and company; to the second, Mr. Bagshot and company; and our hero had the honor and happiness of solely engrossing the third." Set next to the portrait of the erotically posed Tish is a description of her principal gallant:

> The name of this gallant was Tom Smirk. He was clerk to an attorney, and was indeed the greatest beau and the greatest favorite of the ladies at the end of town where he lived. As we take dress to be the characteristic or efficient quality of a beau, we shall, instead of giving any character of this young gentleman, content ourselves with describing his dress only to our readers. He wore, then, a pair of white stockings on his legs, and pumps on his feet; his buckles were a large piece of

pinchbeck plate, which almost covered his whole foot. His breeches were of red plush, which hardly reached his knees; his waistcoat was a white dimity, richly embroidered with yellow silk, over which he wore a blue plush coat with metal buttons, a smart sleeve, with a cape reaching half-way down his back. His wig was of a brown color, covering almost half his pate, on which was hung on one side a little laced hat, but cocked with great smartness. Such was the accomplished Smirk. (Bk. 1, ch. 10)

This beau's function is to satisfy Letty's vanity and so his character is a picture of foppishness, though it is amateurish at best. Indeed, more than any other character, Smirk is a "vice," an embodiment of a traditional sin, vanity (Wild's "greatness" does not belong to an established category of evil). Like Tishy's, the beau's character appears in a closely organized portrait with a clearly marked beginning and end. The detail and varied color of the verbal picture highlight the strained, gaudy, and fashionable exterior of the stereotyped *nouveau-riche* who is striving to attain bourgeois status. The detailed attention directed to his clothes is also employed with a mock-heroic effect. Such descriptions as are reserved in the epic and the romance for great princes and warriors have as their subject an attorney's clerk.

The book's only direct reflection of Smirk's ethos is given in his name, which suggests smug vanity, and his description is a Swiftian equation between dress and soul. Deprived of mind and character, Smirk becomes a rich, overdone façade of clothes. His garish, "fashionable" exterior ironically reflects his empty interior. As an archetype of the vain beau, Smirk is a perfect match for Tishy, the stereotyped, pretentious whore, and her affection for this empty vice is a sly commentary on both figures.

The third person to receive a detailed physical description is Bob Bagshot. A member of Wild's gang, he is also Tishy's lover (she employs him to satisfy her lust), and he is described in this role just after Smirk. This section of *Jonathan Wild*, which is filled with elaborate description, has the aspect of a comic digression. Bagshot is a

> lover, who had all the great and noble qualifications
> necessary to form a true gallant, and which nature is
> seldom so extremely bountiful as to indulge to any one
> person. We will endeavor, however, to describe them
> all with as much exactness as possible. He was then
> six feet high, had large calves, broad shoulders, a ruddy
> complexion, with brown curled hair, a modest assur
> ance, and clean linen. He had indeed, it must be con
> fessed, some small deficiencies to counterbalance those
> heroic qualities, for he was the silliest fellow in the
> world, could neither write nor read, nor had he a
> single grain or spark of honor, honesty, or good-nature
> in his whole composition. (Bk. 1, ch. 12)

This purposefully physical delineation is guided by Bagshot's function; while the fashionable Smirk is rendered in terms of his clothes, Bagshot is described in terms of his physique. Indeed the portrait, by its catalogue of uncovered parts (calves, shoulders, complexion) and its commentary on their adequacy, gives the impression that the man is naked. The incongruous reference to clean linen points up an even more superficial sexual quality. The rendering of Bagshot's physical attributes stands in contrast to the heavy-handed comment on his mental and moral qualities—or rather his lack of them. And although he is presented negatively in terms of his master's central qualities (good nature and honesty), the irony of the novel falters when Fielding calls him "the silliest fellow in the world," momentarily reversing, for the sake of emphasis, the frame of judgment. Despite the two radically different tones, the portrait quite lucidly presents the familiar *machismo* type (Bagshot is devoted to violence), devoid of morality and intelligence.

If it seems curious that only minor characters in *Jonathan Wild* are touched by the pictorial, the reason for this may be found in the fact that, in such a short and tightly controlled work, the major characters bear the responsibility for fulfilling the complex ethical intentions of the apologue. The minor figures are more free because they are less deeply involved in working out the serious themes of the story.[13] Fielding therefore used them to carry the comic interest of his narrative, which they can do without obscuring the principal lines of his moral arguments. Thus Fielding's pictorial descriptions in *Jonathan Wild* are both vehicles for the comedy that surrounds the work's characters and part of larger sexual encounters or scenarios in which the principal motive is comic rather than moral.

III

It should be clear from this discussion that the traditional view of *Jonathan Wild*'s characters as "lifelike individuals," "persons," "human villains," "flesh-and-blood human stuff" cannot be maintained.[14] Our findings, both about the nature of the characters and the patterns in which they are presented (i.e., their relationships with one another), show that the reverse is true. For example, the ties between the figures are not based on natural or personal factors, such as blood or psychological and physical affinities, as in *Amelia*. They are grounded on the relationships among the ideas the figures represent. The main characters, created in various set attitudes around the goodness-greatness question, embody more or less symmetrical points of view in distinct antithesis.[15] Even the minor personages generally form a disciplined, exemplary pattern and are nicely differentiated comic types of good and evil. Taken together, all the characters form ideological *schemas* of closely related positions that completely cover the most important points of the ethical controversy *Jonathan Wild* is built around.

The figures in the apologue are allegorical and semi-allegorical; no attempt is made to create "round" characters in *Jonathan Wild*. The techniques of character delineation are all carefully chosen to emphasize the abstract nature of the figures. Remote historical and mythological persons, like Caesar, Alexander, and Aeneas, are used to provide the reader's perspective on Wild. The biographical character sketch, used to structure the work, is employed because it is ideally suited to depicting representative figures. The result is that, in Wild's case for example, only a few casual incidents (comic in intent) suggest that the hero may not be completely synonymous with greatness. And his antithesis, Heartfree, is nothing if not benevolence itself. All this is only as it should be. Fielding's purpose in *Jonathan Wild* was to explore an ethical rather than a psychological question and to do this in a cerebral manner. His allegorical characters admirably reflect and fulfill this intention.

The development of Fielding's character drawing shows him moving from classical to experimental forms and from characters that embody predominantly intellectual criticism to figures that embody psychological, sentimental comment.[16] *Jonathan Wild* stands at the very beginning of this change. Structured around the formula for the biographical character sketch, it belongs to a classically sanctioned genre in a way that his other prose fiction does not. Its methods of characterization reflect this: all the characters are given significant names, and most are depicted by inherited methods of description, without any attempt to understand individual motivation.

The most pervasive verbal technique of characterization in *Jonathan Wild* is harsh, corrosive irony. All figures are viewed this cerebral way, and there is little comedy in any of the major figures as a result. All the characters, wrought from Fielding's intellectualized system of morality, belong to one of two broad ethical categories, the good or the great. His prime concern is with picturing not affectation but vice in its pure form. At this stage of his development as a character writer, Fielding is quite close to Theophrastus, who was more a moral philosopher than an artist.

The result of Fielding's first attempts at character drawing in prose fiction are more intense than profound, more vigorous than subtle. Yet the cogency of his ethical analysis is always just, and sometimes is penetrating. In itself, this is a substantial achievement.

CHAPTER THREE

Joseph Andrews

*I*N *JONATHAN WILD*, because Fielding wrote largely within a classically sanctioned genre, he employed inherited forms of character depiction in a traditional manner. In *Joseph Andrews*, however, he introduced a new "Species of writing . . . hitherto unattempted in our Language" (preface). It seems natural to assume that this adventurous departure from tradition directly affected his character drawing. But how, and to what degree? We might expect a radical change in the novelist's techniques of characterization. Are such expectations fulfilled? What are the implications of this new form for direct characterization?

I

A look at the intent and structure of *Joseph Andrews* provides us with the first clue to our answers to these questions and suggests that, despite the change in genre, Fielding's character drawing maintained a fundamental continuity with his first work of prose fiction. As in *Jonathan Wild*, he is still fundamentally a moralist, though less direct or more subtle, and instruction is the ultimate purpose behind his work. In consequence, *Joseph Andrews* is didactic (one critic has called it broadly allegorical) and its characters embody, in comic and serious manners, the central moral concerns of the work, described by Martin Battestin as "the exposure of vanity and hypocrisy in society, and the recommendation of their antithetical virtues—charity, chastity, and the classical ideal of life."[1]

On one hand, a small number of characters are selected to recommend Fielding's positive values to the reader. Largely from the lower levels of society, they are exemplars or touchstones who communicate (as the novelist himself says in the opening of *Joseph Andrews*) "valuable Patterns to the World." On the other hand, many characters of all classes (the direct moral antitheses of the ideal patterns) expose worldly vanity and hypocrisy; that is, they are negative patterns or examples of some affectation or vice. The idealized figures are Joseph, Adams, and Fanny; their antitheses are the ubiquitous Didappers, Trullibers, and Slipslops.

Joseph is the first paragon to appear, and his Christian name identifies him with the biblical Joseph, whose rejection of Potiphar's wife made him the proverbial model of chastity both in the Old Testament and in eighteenth-century theological literature. This nominal association and Joseph's chastity establish him as a representation of this virtue, in much the same way as Adams becomes a model of charity.[2]

The first chapter is devoted to a biographical character sketch of Joseph.[3] As the chapter title makes clear, this introductory description is primarily a completion of selected *topoi* from the same rhetorical formula that *Jonathan Wild* is based upon, although here the device is followed less literally and is used more playfully. Fielding even alludes to his use of this formula and draws attention to his casual attitude toward it when he says, ironically: "To waive therefore a Circumstance, which, tho' mentioned in conformity to the exact Rules of Biography, is not greatly material; I proceed to things of more consequence" (bk. 1, ch. 2).

Fielding employs this form in a humorous, mock-heroic manner to set Joseph before the reader in a comic light, using its elevated associations to generate contrast between the mythic figures of the past and their miniature, modern-day counterpart—a footboy, Joey, as he is playfully called.[4] To this end he fills the classical, high-minded *topoi* of the formula with absurd or comic matter, such as the banter about Joseph's relationship to "that Sect of laughing Philosophers, since called *Merry Andrews*." At other times Fielding confesses, with playful embarrassment, that there is nothing with which to complete the "places." Speaking about the hero's ancestors (a central category in the formula), Fielding says: "As to his Ancestors, we have searched with great Diligence but little Success" (bk. 1, ch. 2). The ironic contrast between the high vehicle and the comic matter, or rather the complete lack of matter of any kind, reflects satirically on Joseph, suggesting rustic, unsophisticated, and obscure origins at the same time that it prepares for the identity crisis at the end of the novel. Maintaining its comic tone, this introductory description moves from the conventional biographical formula to a chronological narrative of significant events in Joseph's life, chosen to illustrate his basic good nature. The youth's life story is swiftly brought up to the point at which the novel opens, and the writer turns to sketch Adams.

Although the opening biographical sketch of the novel is the first description of Joseph Andrews, it is not the only one. In book 1, chapter 8, there is a quite different description of the hero:

> Mr. *Joseph Andrews* was now in the one and twentieth Year of his Age. He was of the highest Degree of middle Stature. His Limbs were put together with great Elegance and no less Strength. His Legs and Thighs were formed in the exactest Proportion. His Shoulders were broad and brawny, but yet his Arms hung so easily, that he had all the Symptoms of Strength without the least clumsiness. His Hair was of a nutbrown Colour, and was displayed in wanton Ringlets down his Back. His Forehead was high, his Eyes dark, and as full of Sweetness as of Fire. His Nose a little inclined to the Roman. His Teeth white and even. His Lips full, red, and soft. His Beard was only rough on his Chin and upper Lip; but his Cheeks, in which his Blood glowed, were overspread with a thick Down. His Countenance had a Tenderness joined with a Sensibility inexpressible. Add to this the most perfect Neatness in his Dress, and an Air, which to those who have not seen many Noblemen, would give an Idea of Nobility.

This detailed physical description, which focuses almost exclusively on Joseph's body and so makes him into something of a sex object, is withheld until Lady Booby attempts to seduce her footman, when it is subtly appropriate. As Fielding observes: "Such was the Person [i.e., body] who now appeared before the Lady. She viewed him some time in Silence, and twice or thrice before she spake." By implication, we understand that this rather selective picture of Joseph, if it is not actually a function of Lady Booby's aroused imagination, is at least similar to the image of him that makes her so uneasy. In addition to giving us a certain view of Joseph, this sensuous picture is an important part of the novel's principal seduction scene. Like other aspects of that scene (the bedroom setting and the teasing questions of Lady Booby, for example), the picture contributes to the intense and pervasive sexual air that envelops the episode.

Fielding's description of Joseph is also guided by the traditional methods of previous literary portraiture: first the full stature of the hero is described; then his frame is viewed, limb by limb, in the manner of the Renaissance portrait. At the conclusion, just before the writer moves from *stasis* to action, the hero's figure is seen in its totality. Throughout the idealized description, which, unlike Fanny's, is devoid of motion, Joseph is set in a pose similar to that adopted by the subject of a full-length eighteenth-century portrait. Of course, he is also standing attentively at the bedside of his mistress and is viewed through her idealizing eyes.

The primary focus of depiction is the face. While other parts of Joseph's form are presented in a perfunctory way, the descriptive method slows abruptly as the novelist paints the hero's countenance detail by detail. Again, the head is consistently described as if it were posed for a painting, and the hero appears to be looking to one side (his nose inclines to the Roman). However, it is not just the pose that is pictorial; presented in short, breathless phrases, the details are rich and full and are described in a variety of colors, some of which are characteristic of portrait painting at and before Fielding's time. In the most prominent tradition of the visual arts of the age, all the features of the hero (with the exception of his nose) are conventionally perfect and harmonious, presenting a coherent and highly idealized picture of Joseph Andrews. Joseph's portrait seems designed to give us two distinct impressions about the young man's nature that balance and temper each other. The first part of the delineation, which outlines the hero's "person," emphasizes his brawny masculinity, youthful strength, and athletic vigor. Described with consciously erotic details (wanton ringlets; eyes of fire; full, red, soft lips), Joseph's head and countenance tell about a different part of his nature. By means of these conventional sexual qualities the hero's deeply sensual nature (which later is more completely revealed in his relationship with Fanny) is broached. Here, more than anywhere else, the reader sees Joseph through the eyes of the tormented Lady Booby.

A number of critics have remarked on the physical similarity between Joseph and Fanny and a literal comparison confirms that observation.

Joseph	*Fanny*
"His Hair was of a nut-brown Colour"	"Her Hair was of a Chestnut Brown"
"His Forehead was high"	"Her Forehead was high"
"His Eyes dark"	"Her Eyes black"
"His Nose a little inclined to the Roman"	"Her Nose, just inclining to the *Roman*"
"His Lips full, red, and soft"	"Her Lips red and moist"
"His Teeth white and even"	"Her Teeth were white, but not exactly even"
"His Countenance had a Tenderness joined with a Sensibility inexpressible"	"Add to these, a Countenance in which . . . a Sensibility appeared almost incredible"

Some scholars have suggested that Fielding described Joseph in feminine terms to satirize his priggish and fastidious sexual morality, seeing his feminine appearance as emblematic of the reversal of the male-female roles in Joseph's interaction with Lady Booby. And there can be little doubt that Fielding plays with the comic aspects of the "Character of Male-Chastity" that Joseph adopts at this point. No libertine himself, nor yet a great admirer of male chastity, it was Fielding's constant practice to introduce breaches of middle-class sexual morality by both sexes as a venial sin.[5] Still, this ingenious account connecting the hero's passivity with his feminine appearance does not explain what Fielding is doing. The real significance of Joseph's appearance and remarkable similarity to Fanny is to be found in the standards of male beauty and attractiveness that were in vogue from the Renaissance to the eighteenth century. As the portraits of Restoration and Augustan noblemen suggest, Joseph's "effeminacy" was a desirable quality in young men of that age. Characteristically believed to be an aristocratic mark, it was valued as a civilizing factor that tempered the purely robust and was thought to distinguish the nobleman from the peasant.

For all the details in his portrait, nothing is said about Joseph's character, and nothing need be said.[6] In his "Essay on the Knowledge of the Characters of Men," Fielding wrote that the passions commonly imprint sufficient marks on the countenance to indicate their presence. "Nature," Fielding said, "which unwillingly submits to the imposture, is ever endeavouring to peep forth and show herself; nor can the cardinal, the friar, or the judge, long conceal the sot, the gamester, or the rake" (14: 283). Thus, he claims, gravity or austerity of countenance

indicates pride, ill nature, and cunning; a sneer indicates malice and fraud. A bully is betrayed by a fierce
aspect while an amiable, open, composed, cheerful countenance infallibly signals a good heart and conscience.
Later in this essay Fielding warns that his theory has
limited application in life, but this is not true in his novels.[7]
Granted the villain's limited ability to control his facial
responses, the countenance of a character is a reliable
index to his or her nature. Of Joseph we are told: "His
Countenance had a Tenderness joined with a Sensibility
inexpressible." In a word, his idealized appearance mir-
rors his moral and psychological perfection. The details
of this self-evident perfection are to be learned from his
actions.

Fielding has often been praised for the subtle ways in
which he prepares the reader for the "surprise" ending in
Tom Jones, although the same skillful preparation for the
conclusion of *Joseph Andrews* has gone unnoticed. The
vague manner in which Joseph's origins are related ("[he]
was *esteemed* to be the only Son" [italics mine]) was
certainly noticed by acute readers. Furthermore, Fielding's educated readers would have recognized that the
mode in which Joseph is described was traditionally used
to present heroes of rank and noble birth in Renaissance
literature.[8] For readers who might have missed the implications of status, Fielding concludes Joseph's portrait
by noting his "Air, which to those who have not seen
many Noblemen, would give an Idea of Nobility."
Indeed, at least one person in the novel is alert to the significance of his appearance: Betty the chambermaid (who
scrutinizes the hero's skin with particular closeness, we
may be sure), proclaims "he was a Gentleman: for she
never saw a finer Skin in her Life" (bk. 1, ch. 14). And

what was previously implicit is made explicit: the hero is not a fellow of low birth—Mr. Wilson describes himself as descended of "a good Family and . . . born a Gentleman."

The final line in Joseph's description is more than subtle praise and an indication of his high birth; it is also a Swiftian statement about the physical vitality of the working classes as opposed to the debilitated real-life aristocracy. As such, it is an interesting indication of Fielding's ambivalent attitude toward the nobility. Although he felt he must make Joseph a gentleman to vindicate him, he condemns the vitiated ruling class. In addition, this line may well be a hit at Richardson's naïveté about the upper classes, as some scholars have suggested.[9] Finally, it seems that Fielding makes this point about the degeneracy of the aristocracy to prepare his readers for Joseph's foil—in the person of a nobleman who is later introduced in direct antithesis (both moral and physical) to the hero.

This person is beau Didapper, who appears toward the end of *Joseph Andrews* in the role (as he and Lady Booby conceive it) of Joseph's rival for Fanny's love. Didapper's appearance is described in the following manner:

> Mr. *Didapper*, or Beau *Didapper*, was a young Gentleman of about four Foot five Inches in height. He wore his own Hair, tho' the Scarcity of it might have given him sufficient Excuse for a Periwig. His Face was thin and pale: The Shape of his Body and Legs none of the best; for he had very narrow Shoulders, and no Calf; and his Gait might more properly be called hopping than walking. (Bk. 4, ch. 9)

The beau's appearance is a Hogarthian distortion and reversal of Joseph's idealized face and masculine physique.

Joseph is "of the highest Degree of middle Stature"; Didapper is "about four Foot five Inches in height." The legs and thighs of our hero are "formed in the exactest Proportion," whereas the beau's body and legs are "none of the best; for he had very narrow Shoulders, and no Calf." Introduced when Didapper appears, in Joseph's presence, to present his suit to Fanny, his neatly reversed description and its appropriateness to the contrast between the two men is a good illustration of Fielding's ability to use visual detail for ironic comment.

The beau's continental propensities (he can speak French and he assumes the title "beau") suggest that the source for his description may be the affected Frenchman in Hogarth's *Noon*.[10] Both, certainly, have much in common: a cane, fine clothes, an affected gait. Even their physical appearance is similar: both are small and have feminine mannerisms, weak legs, and narrow shoulders. But despite these similarities there are not enough details to establish Hogarth's Frenchman as Fielding's incontrovertible source. Undoubtedly the novelist noticed the artist's figure, and very probably some of the visual elements of Didapper's portrait (his cane, clothes, and hopping gait) derive from Hogarth.

If Fielding's precise use of Hogarth's print must remain unclear, his employment of another visual tradition is more obvious. The didapper is a dab-chick or small water bird that is "characterized by a short body, flattened and webbed feet set far behind, and the virtual absence of tail."[11] In the seventeenth and eighteenth centuries there was an occult belief in the sexual ambivalence of the didapper: it was described as "equivocally produced."[12] As a consequence, the bird became a symbol for bisexuality and asexuality[13]—qualities that this and many later generations found so threatening that they ridiculed rather than examined and accepted them.

This dab-chick is the controlling image in Fielding's description of Mr. Didapper. The water bird is emblematically conceived and the beau is presented in terms of the physical and moral characteristics associated with the fowl. The description of the beau is composed of details that were selected to convey the dab-chick allusion to the reader with economy and precision. Didapper is small, has birdlike legs ("no Calf") and does not walk but "hops." He has the same ambiguous sexual nature as his namesake: he is "so little subject to Lust, that he had, among those who knew him best, the Character of great Moderation in his Pleasures" (bk. 4, ch. 9). His assault on the voluptuous Fanny soon leaves him out of breath and he leaves her to a servant who has "more warm Blood about him than his Master" (bk. 4, ch. 7). Perhaps guided by Hogarth's effete Frenchman, Fielding shapes, modifies, and exploits details of natural appearance to give an evocative emblematic dimension of his figure.

Fielding concluded his depiction of Didapper with a genuinely negative account, which is followed by an ironic, positive account of his mental qualities:

> The Qualifications of his Mind were well adapted to his Person. We shall handle them first negatively. He was not entirely ignorant: For he could talk a little *French*, and sing two or three *Italian* Songs: He had lived too much in the World to be bashful, and too much at Court to be proud: He seemed not much inclined to Avarice; for he was profuse in his Expences: Nor had he all the Features of Prodigality; for he never gave a Shilling:—No Hater of Women; for he always dangled after them; yet so little subject to Lust, that he had,

among those who knew him best, the Character of great Moderation in his Pleasures. No Drinker of Wine; nor so addicted to Passion, but that a hot Word or two from an Adversary made him immediately cool. (Bk. 4, ch. 9)

This passage, and the one to follow, are remarkable among Fielding's descriptions of character because they overtly identify Didapper with a contemporary. The portrayal of the beau as a dab-chick and his delineation as ignorant, avaricious, cowardly, and of ambiguous sexual persuasion seem to refer both to the character of Lord Hervey and to Pope's picture of him as Sporus—the amphibious, effeminate bug "Whose Buzz the Witty and the Fair annoys, Yet Wit ne'er tastes, and Beauty ne'er enjoys."

Didapper's equally damning positive qualities point with telling specificity in the same direction:

Now, to give him only a Dash or two on the affirmative Side: 'Tho' he was born to an immense Fortune, he chose, for the pitiful and dirty Consideration of a Place of little consequence, to depend entirely on the Will of a Fellow, whom they call a Great-Man; who treated him with the utmost Disrespect, and exacted of him a plenary Obedience to his Commands; which he implicitly submitted to, at the Expence of his Conscience, his Honour, and of his Country; in which he had himself so very large a Share.' And to finish his Character, 'As he was entirely well satisfied with his own Person and Parts, so he was very apt to ridicule and laugh at any Imperfection in another.' Such was the little Person or rather Thing that hopped after Lady *Booby* into Mr. *Adams'* kitchin. (Ibid.)

This passage leaves the identity of the beau beyond dispute.

The first part of the biographical sketch is Fielding's condensation and inversion of two paragraphs from Conyers Middleton's dedication to Lord Hervey in his *Life of Cicero*. Fielding adapted these paragraphs from Middleton's description of Hervey's patriotism by echoing the phrasing at the beginning and end of this encomium. The second part of the passage (in quotation marks) is a paraphrase of two statements from Pope's privately circulated "Letter to a Noble Lord" which satirized Hervey under the title "Fannius."[14] The last line refers to the emblematic description of the beau and, through the use of "thing" and "hopped," strengthens the image of Didapper as a water bird. This unique use of biographical details about the notorious Lord Hervey to complete Didapper's portrait is a clever, comic stroke. This real-life material makes the sketch's generalized attack on the nobility plausible because the portrait is self-validating, containing its own empirical proof.

The second figure in the novel who functions as a negative embodiment that enables us to judge Joseph's values is Mr. Wilson, the subject of the extended character sketch that is the longest digression in *Joseph Andrews*. This involved sketch, organized to suggest a single character, is initially similar in form to the conventional biographies in other parts of the novel. Fielding begins by having Wilson recite his ancestry, parentage, and education, but then he turns the sketch into an apologue that surveys, in didactic fashion, the vices and corruption of life in the city, which Joseph, because of his virtue, has been cast out of. Most of this apologue consists of common scenes from London life, represented in a manner which parallels, imitates, and evokes the most vivid engravings of Fielding's artist friend Hogarth, whose moralizing statements on urban life were familiar to most of the novelist's readers.[15] The organization of this portrait and its references to Hogarth's scenes are quite varied. In general, Wilson's life follows *A Rake's Progress* in all but its final scene. Between the stages of Wilson's degeneration is material of Fielding's own devising, as well as material from other plates of Hogarth, notably *A Harlot's Progress*. At the conclusion of Fielding's tale, however, his protagonist—by an unlikely but Fieldingesque turn of events—goes not to Bedlam but to a cottage in the country with his new wife.

The details of Wilson's early life are taken from London life as they were methodized by the engraver. Wilson, like Rakewell in plate 1 of *A Harlot's Progress*, is descended from a good family and at a young age came to London from a public school, because his father had died and left him a fortune.[16] The central action in Hogarth's plates is reflected in Wilson's words: "The Character I was ambitious of attaining, was that of a fine Gentleman; the first Requisites to which, I apprehended were to be supplied by a Taylor, a Periwig-maker, and some few more Tradesmen, who deal in furnishing out the human body" (bk. 3, ch. 3). Immediately after this, Wilson mimics the ideals of a gentleman as they appear in Rakewell's levee (plate 2 of *A Rake's Progress*). "The next Qualifications, namely Dancing, Fencing, Riding the great Horse, and Musick, came into my head." For these scenes Adams, and sometimes Wilson himself (as proof of his reformation), supply recurring exclamations which serve as captions to the novel's pictures. "*Good Lord!*" says Adams after the first scenes, "*What wicked Times these are?*"·

At this point Fielding departs briefly from his direct

evocation of Hogarth; when he returns, it is to *A Harlot's Progress*. Describing Wilson's attempt to keep a whore, Fielding's narration not only reproduces exact figures from Hogarth (the celebrated bawd and the city apprentice of plate 2) but invests them with Hogarth's poses and characteristic details. The young man is dressed like an officer and the whore is snapping her fingers and rapping out oaths at her keeper. Here is the scene in full: Having decided to keep a whore, Wilson

> fixed my Choice on a young Woman, who had before been kept by two Gentlemen, and to whom I was recommended by a celebrated Bawd. I took her to my Chambers, and made her a Settlement, during Cohabitation. This would perhaps have been very ill paid: However, she did not suffer me to be perplexed on that account; for before Quarter-day, I found her at my Chambers in too familiar Conversation with a young Fellow who was drest like an Officer, but was indeed a City Apprentice. Instead of excusing her Inconstancy, she rapped out half a dozen Oaths, and snapping her Fingers at me, swore she scorned to confine herself to the best Man in *England*. Upon this we parted. (Bk. 3, ch. 3)

Fielding's protagonist then seduces a widow's daughter, and the "progress" of this girl also seems to be related to *A Harlot's Progress*. Again, although the material is commonplace, the evocation of Hogarth is clear. Like Moll (in plate 1), Wilson's mistress is described as "a beautiful young Girl" and "a fine young Creature"; however, she is introduced to degenerate company and begins "to play at Cards, and frequent Plays and other Diversions [masquerades?]." Again like Moll, "all her Modesty and Innocence vanished by degrees, till her Mind became thoroughly tainted. She affected the Company of Rakes, gave herself all manners of Airs, was never easy but abroad, or when she had a Party at my Chambers." She then parts with her keeper, becomes a whore, and dies in prison: "Indeed I could wish I had never heard more of the poor Creature, who became in the end an abandoned Profligate; and after being some Years a common Prostitute, at last ended her miserable Life in *Newgate*" (bk. 3, ch. 3).

After a few more affairs with women, Wilson joins the characters in another Hogarth plate. "I fell," he tells us, "into the Acquaintance of a Set of jolly Companions, who slept all Day, and drank all Night: Fellows who might rather be said to consume Time than to live. Their best Conversation was nothing but Noise: Singing, Hollowing, Wrangling, Drinking, Toasting, Sp-wing, Smoking, were the chief Ingredients of our Entertainment" (bk. 3, ch. 3). All the essential elements of *A Midnight Modern Conversation* are here, and in this plate the same type of people (jolly companions) are indulging in the same activity (drinking) at the same time (all night). Beyond this, the same breakdown of activities within Hogarth's print is reflected in Fielding's writing. In *A Modern Conversation*, most of the characters are smoking and drinking; one is toasting; two are wrangling; one is singing; and one is spewing. None of the action in Hogarth's print is ignored by Fielding. The rest of Wilson's life follows the general lines of *A Rake's Progress*. Arrested and imprisoned for debt, he attempts to make money by writing a play, but it is rejected. Finally he is rescued by the sudden and unlikely appearance of a Sarah Young figure, who marries him, and they go off to the country to bring up a family.

This biography is primarily an attack upon the evils Fielding believed to be almost inherent in city life. It was made with the assistance of Hogarth, whose imagination was considerably more negative than Fielding's and whose work evokes a grotesque, pessimistic mood of its own, together with a profoundly deterministic morality. In this sense the biography is a completion of the description and satire of urban life that began with Joseph's taking up residence in London.

In addition, the character of Wilson—as it is developed with Hogarth's guidance—provides an instructive contrast to that of Joseph, his son. Joseph, a member of the serving class, raised in the country, and educated by Parson Adams, does not lose his native integrity, not even in London. Wilson, on the other hand, is educated at a public school, is raised without Christian guidance, and most important of all, aspires like Rakewell to a higher class, and so becomes embroiled in the corruption of city life. His lack of a religious guide is also of special significance, and Wilson himself remarks on it: "to this early Introduction into Life, without a Guide, I impute all my future Misfortunes" (bk. 3, ch. 3).

Wilson's sketch is a background which establishes the importance of Adams's life and teaching for Joseph—and by extension the importance of a good Christian example and education. It also helps provide a perspective on the life and values of the novel's hero. Initially, for example, Joseph's zealous chastity seems mildly ludicrous, but when we see the confused, predatory sexuality that the novelist suggests as the alternative, we see the hero's strict moral integrity in a new light. Likewise, the footman's irreligious behavior and foppish vanity seem even less serious than they did earlier. Joseph's judgment of city life ("London is a bad Place"), his desire to return to the country (which he implicitly judges to be the repository of superior values), and the semipastoral qualities in the rural life of the "new" Wilson are all affirmed in this character sketch.

II

Parson Adams, the "good man" in the novel and its central ethical voice, appears immediately after Joseph,[17] and the use of his full name suggests his character. In the theological literature of the age, the biblical Abraham was commonly offered by latitudinarian divines as a model of charity that was worthy of imitation. Therefore, as Martin Battestin suggests, Fielding called his clergyman Abraham to establish him as the novel's good-natured man and made him both a model of virtue and a comic analogue of the Old Testament patriarch. The parson's surname links him with the first human being and Adam's reputed natural innocence and simplicity.

Abraham Adams is depicted by a passage of psychological characterization that is devoid of Fielding's customary irony. The sketch is among the novel's most abstract. Nothing is said about Adams's physical appearance; he is described only in terms of his intellectual and moral qualities.

> Mr. *Abraham Adams* was an excellent Scholar. He was a perfect Master of the Greek and Latin Languages; to which he added a great Share of Knowledge in the Oriental Tongues, and could read and translate *French*, *Italian* and *Spanish*. He had applied many Years to the most severe Study, and had treasured up a Fund of

Learning rarely to be met with in a University." (Bk.
1, ch. 3)

This passage, which describes Adams as an academic, is
the first of a number of keys to his character. He lives in
a world of Greek and Roman writers that is more real to
him than England itself. The lack of contemporary awareness in Adams, together with a number of idiosyncrasies
and peccadilloes (he is vain about his learning, unrealistic
about its relevance and, like most of Fielding's heroes, is
naïve about his own nature and human nature in general),
makes him fallible and human—not sufficiently perfect to
be, like Allworthy, an embodied ethical concept.

Adams's moral qualities are even more impressive than
his extraordinary learning.

> He was besides a Man of good Sense, good Parts, and
> good Nature; but was at the same time as entirely ig-
> norant of the Ways of this World, as an Infant just
> entered into it could possibly be. As he had never any
> Intention to deceive, so he never suspected such a De-
> sign in others. He was generous, friendly and brave to
> an Excess; but Simplicity was his Characteristic. (Ibid.)

His "good nature" and "simplicity," together with his
generosity and charity, strengthen the parson's association
with the patriarch Abraham. His simplicity (Fielding remarks in the preface that Adams is intended to be the
"character of perfect Simplicity") is to be understood
primarily in a theological sense, for "simplicity" was
used during the eighteenth century in Theophrastan character books and religious writing to describe artless, unaffected dispositions which were free from deceit and
duplicity. Thus we are to see Adams as a plain, blunt

---

person of the highest integrity and also as a naïve, other-worldly figure whose idealism is exceeded only by his innocence, which permits him to function in a satiric role by passing implicit judgments on the immorality around him.

There is an instructive contrast between the way Adams is conceived in this sketch and how he is realized in the plot. Abstract and theoretical, the description of the parson is remote and lifeless. Moreover, it is misleading to describe him as "a Man of good Sense." But thrust into the action of the novel, Adams far exceeds the expectations of his prosaic depiction; he becomes not only the most human and delightfully vital of all the mentors in Fielding's novels but "one of the few completely engaging representations in fiction of a good Christian."[18]

Adams is not only the moral center of the novel but the foil to half a dozen other clergymen who represent various degrees and kinds of corruption common to ecclesiastics.[19] There is the litigious rector, who is Adams's superior; the slothful, punch-drinking Barnabas, whom Adams meets on the road; and the grossly ignorant country parson, who thinks Adams's *Aeschylus* is "the Catechism in Greek" (bk. 2, ch. 11). But the most memorable clergyman is presented in a brief set piece: Reverend Mr. Trulliber. It is entirely appropriate that this parson, juxtaposed to the spiritual Adams, should be a coarse, earthy fellow.

Mr. *Trulliber* was a Parson on *Sundays*, but all the other six might more properly be called a Farmer. He occupied a small piece of Land of his own, besides which he rented a considerable deal more. His Wife milked his Cows, managed his Dairy, and followed the Markets with Butter and Eggs. The Hogs fell chiefly to his care,

which he carefully waited on at home, and attended to
Fairs; on which occasion he was liable to many Jokes,
his own Size being with much Ale rendered little inferiour to that of the Beasts he sold. He was indeed one
of the largest Men you should see, and could have acted
the part of Sir *John Falstaff* without stuffing. Add to
this, that the Rotundity of his Belly was considerably
increased by the shortness of his Stature, his Shadow
ascending very near as far in height when he lay on his
Back, as when he stood on his Legs. His Voice was loud
and hoarse, and his Accents extremely broad; to complete the whole, he had a Stateliness in his Gate, when
he walked, not unlike that of a Goose, only he stalked
slower. (Bk. 2, ch. 14)

In the seventeenth and eighteenth centuries the hog
was a recognized symbol of greed and self-indulgence.
The *Oxford English Dictionary* shows that "hog" sig-
nified "a coarse, self-indulgent, gluttonous, or filthy person" from 1436 through the eighteenth century, and
Ripa's *Iconologia: or Moral Emblems*, popular in the
eighteenth century,[20] portrays gluttony as a woman with
a big belly standing beside a hog. Ripa's text is even more
explicit: "The Hog imports *Gluttony*."[21] Fielding, in
turn, makes Trulliber a Ripa-like emblem for gluttony
by having the farmer-parson resemble his hogs as closely
as natural detail will permit.

Trulliber's name, moreover, is a latinized form of the
colloquial "trullibub," a variant of "trillibub," which
means the entrails or innards of an animal, and the word
was commonly used as a jeering appellation for a fat
man.[22] Emphasizing Trulliber's large belly, the name also
identifies him with Ripa's allegorical figure by pointing
up the striking similarity between pig and parson, which

becomes more explicit as the description unfolds. Trulliber is "with much Ale rendered little inferiour [in appearance] to that of the Beasts he sold." But it is his posture, frame, and voice that leave no doubt about the comparison. His belly is huge and his stature short, and when he lies on his back (a position more common to hogs in a sty than to a parson) he seems much the same size as when he stands.

In a recent article on Trulliber (to which I am indebted) Douglas Brooks suggests that Fielding associated the parson-farmer with gluttony by describing him as a crane (another emblem for gluttony) and making him a hog keeper. He suggests that Trulliber is also associated with Bacchus because the second part of his name, "liber," is Latin for Bacchus. Brooks's basic point about the identification of Trulliber with gluttony is undoubtedly sound, but the Bacchus and crane identifications seem too remote from the text. Fielding certainly renders Trulliber in the pose suggested by the icon, but he does it not by juxtaposing the pig and the man but by having the man simulate the pig in appearance, sound and conduct. The parson, closely resembling a hog, becomes an emblem for gluttony and indulgence because of his visual and mythic associations with that animal. By exploiting resemblances that are comic and emblematic, Fielding created a figure that is both natural in appearance and semiallegorical in nature.

III

Fanny, the female paragon in *Joseph Andrews*, is the novel's and the eighteenth-century male world's moral and physical ideal of womanhood, and the yardstick by which Lady Booby, Slipslop, and Tow-wouse (her rivals for Joseph's love)—and of course Pamela—are to be judged. In contrast to the prolific and voluble Pamela in Richardson's *Pamela*, Fanny's part in *Joseph Andrews* is limited: she is only intermittently verbal and very seldom active. The occasions on which she is prominent are central to her function in the novel as a surpassingly beautiful but passive image of good nature and chastity.

Fanny is not described when she first enters the novel; her presentation is withheld until just before Joseph is reunited with her so that the reader may feel the same combination of awe and transport as the hero. Like Joseph, she is presented in a set-piece literary portrait.

> *Fanny* was now in the nineteenth Year of her Age; she was tall and delicately shaped; but not one of those slender young Women, who seem rather intended to hang up in the Hall of an Anatomist, than for any other Purpose. On the contrary, she was so plump, that she seemed bursting through her tight Stays, especially in the Part which confined her swelling Breasts. Nor did her Hips want the Assistance of a Hoop to extend them. The exact Shape of her Arms, denoted the Form of those Limbs which she concealed; and tho' they were a little redden'd by her Labour, yet if her Sleeve slipt above her Elbow, or her Handkerchief discovered any part of her Neck, a Whiteness appeared which the finest *Italian* Paint would be unable to reach. Her Hair was of a Chestnut Brown, and Nature had been extremely lavish to her of it, which she had cut, and on *Sundays* used to curl down her Neck in the modern Fashion. Her Forehead was high, her Eye-brows arched, and rather full than otherwise. Her Eyes black and sparkling; her Nose, just inclining to the *Roman;* her Lips red and moist, and her Under-Lip, according to the Opinion of the Ladies, too pouting. Her Teeth

were white, but not exactly even. The Small-Pox had left one only Mark on her Chin, which was so large, it might have been mistaken for a Dimple, had not her left Cheek produced one so near a Neighbour to it, that the former served only for a Foil to the latter. Her Complexion was fair, a little injured by the Sun, but overspread with such a Bloom, that the finest Ladies would have exchanged all their White for it: add to these, a Countenance in which tho' she was extremely bashful, a Sensibility appeared almost incredible; and a Sweetness, whenever she smiled, beyond either Imitation or Description. To conclude all, she had a natural Gentility, superior to the Acquisition of Art, and which surprized all who beheld her. (Bk. 2, ch. 12)

This elaborate portrait presents Fanny in the tradition of the idealized Renaissance lady to emphasize the contrast between her simple, rustic origins and circumstances and her natural gentility. Perhaps Fielding wanted to suggest about her the sentiments Lady Brooks expresses in *Pamela:* "See that shape! . . . why, she must be better descended that you have told me." At any rate, Fanny's lineage is clearly of less importance to Fielding, because she is a woman and will marry a gentleman.[23] Very much a part of this emphasis on the heroine's natural gentility is the unmistakable full-length portrait that seems to accompany this description.

Fielding himself refers to the sketch not as a "character" (his usual term), but as a "picture." Its organization is emphatically visual; it is framed by a formally marked beginning and end. Within these limits the portrait develops organically in terms of an obvious and consistent relationship to a pictorial source, as does the tradition it follows. The statements about Fanny are visually conceived and are rich in such pictorial details as color and line, and the characteristic quality of the sketch is *stasis*. Although there is just a suggestion of motion in Fielding's description of Fanny's arm and neck, her figure, and particularly her face, are fixed in a static pose and it is against this static organization that any motion must be seen. Even the language asserts the pictorial nature of the description: Fanny's white skin is compared to "the finest *Italian* Paint."[24]

Whether Fanny is modeled on a figure from the visual arts is more difficult to tell. The ideal silhouette of fashion in the visual arts in Fielding's time is codified and illustrated in Boucher's painting *Madame de Pompadour* (signed and dated 1759), in which the body is an inverted cone or triangle, the breasts are suppressed, and the waist and neck are equally narrow.[25] There can be no doubt that Fielding specifically rejected this fashionable model in describing Fanny as "not one of those slender young Women, who seem rather intended to hang up in the Hall of an Anatomist." He mentions, with approval, the fullness of her breasts, and throughout makes the reader aware of her solid, plump, well-rounded body just beneath the sleeve or kerchief.

Fielding's emphasis on healthy corporality rejects all the forms and aids of art. Fanny is a child of nature, whom art can neither define nor represent properly, any more than hoops can flatter her hips or "*Italian* Paint" can reveal her tone of skin. When he first sees Fanny's naked body, Joseph, who has some familiarity with the visual arts, says, "All the Statues he ever beheld were so much inferiour to it in Beauty, that it was more capable of converting a Man into a Statue, than of being imitated by the greatest Master of that Art" (bk. 4, ch. 7).

When Fielding describes the heroine's countenance, however, he relies more on art than on nature. Fanny's curly hair (and Joseph's as well, which is the same in all respects) and its chestnut brown color are characteristic of Italian portraiture, and Fielding's mention of Italian paint suggests that he had that tradition in mind when he wrote. The other facial features are taken, as in many idealized descriptions, from a concept of nature that had been formulated by Renaissance literary practices. A departure from oppressive idealization is the heroine's Roman nose, uneven teeth, sunburned complexion, smallpox mark, and labor-reddened arms, which are added to the description to reveal Fanny's class origins. These tiny flaws also individualize her somewhat and temper her beauty without changing her status. And although these imperfections represent a move toward formal realism in Fielding's treatment of appearance, his description is guided by the principle of decorum, which holds that depiction must aim not at external reality but at matching the mode of portrayal to the status of the portrayed. Fanny's portrait ends with a summarizing statement, climactic and superlative, affirming that her beauty is emblematic of her good nature: her face tells of her sensibility and sweetness; her natural gentility is beyond the reach of art.

Most of the women in the novel operate as foils to the morally and physically idealized heroine. The lascivious Lady Booby, the haughty Pamela, and the warm-blooded Betty are contrasted with different virtuous traits in the heroine. And two particularly grotesque figures are singled out by Fielding to serve in more direct contrast to Fanny in both the moral and the physical realm: Slipslop and Tow-wouse.

The first of these figures to appear in the novel is Slip-slop,[26] whose name is indicative both of her habitual malapropisms (many of which are delightful Freudian slips that expose her lewdness) and her lustful nature. Here is her portrait, introduced just prior to her attempted seduction of Joseph to add to the comic incongruity of that act.

> She was a Maiden Gentlewoman of about Forty-five Years of Age, who having made a small Slip in her Youth had continued a good Maid ever since. She was not at this time remarkably handsome; being very short, and rather too corpulent in Body, and somewhat red, with the Addition of Pimples in the Face. Her Nose was likewise rather too large, and her Eyes too little; nor did she resemble a Cow so much in her Breath, as in the two brown Globes which she carried before her; one of her Legs was also a little shorter than the other, which occasioned her to limp as she walked. (Bk. 1, ch. 6)

This portrait is an interesting contrast to the picture of Fanny, as both descriptions are purposefully antithetic. Fanny has delicate, idealized features and a robust, healthy form; Slipslop, on the other hand, has a coarse, grotesque appearance and a corpulent, disproportionate body. Again, Fielding's theory of physiognomy is at work: the maid's bovine form and pimpled face, with its small eyes, are outward signs of her gross, animal lusts and her circumscribed powers of perception.

In form as well, this verbal picture is different from Fanny's. The dignified formal description, portraitlike in manner, is not employed and the Hogarthian Slipslop is described by a few suggestive visual details. Her shape and appearance are calculated to suggest physical similarity to a cow, and thus her short stature, bovine corpulence and coloring, and large nose. And lest the importance of these features be missed, the similarity is made explicit by the serving woman's udderlike breasts.

Although the cow is not a visual emblem in the works of Cesare Ripa, the *Oxford English Dictionary* suggests that it was thought of as a literary or mythological emblem and defines it as "applied to a coarse or degraded woman." Quoting from *A New World of English Words* (1696), the *Oxford English Dictionary* cites Edward Phillips's definition of the cow as the "Emblem . . . of a Lazy, Dronish, beastly Woman, who is likened to a Cow." Fielding, obviously, exploited this emblematic use in describing Slipslop. Emphasizing the natural resemblances, the novelist provides more than a general indication of her appearance. Creating her in the image of a cow, Fielding identifies her with that emblem and with its associated moral qualities: sloth and animality.

Fanny's second rival for Joseph is the niggardly virago Mrs. Tow-wouse, the keeper of the Dragon Inn. The words that make up her name are not recorded in the *Oxford English Dictionary*, but "Tow-wow" appeared in a pamphlet in 1725 with the same meaning as *comment-a-nom*, or "as it is called"—a non-specific euphemism. The lady is introduced and described after her verbal attack on the coachman, who left the injured, but worse still, penniless Joseph at her inn. It is made explicit that her countenance is indicative of her disposition.

Her Person was short, thin, and crooked. Her Forehead projected in the middle, and thence descended in a Declivity to the Top of her Nose, which was sharp and red, and would have hung over her Lips, had not Nature turned up the end of it. Her Lips were two Bits of Skin, which, whenever she spoke, she drew together in a Purse. Her Chin was peeked, and at the upper end of that Skin, which composed her Cheeks, stood two Bones, that almost hid a Pair of small red Eyes. Add to this, a Voice most wonderfully adapted to the Sentiments it was to convey, being both loud and hoarse. (Bk. 1, ch. 14)

With brief, sure strokes the novelist depicts Mrs. Towwouse. In describing her face, Fielding reflects the importance of the countenance in current artistic practice by representing his subject in a state of complete *stasis*, but he does not employ his usual ordered and comprehensive enumeration. Selecting very prominent facial features, he describes their visual qualities (detail, line, color) in an order that brings the entire face to the mind's eye simultaneously. It is difficult to believe (especially since Fielding associates Hogarth's name with this portrait) that the grotesque spirit of the face does not owe some of its graphic quality to Fielding's familiarity with Mrs. Towwouse's many caricatured analogues in Hogarth's prints.

Mrs. Tow-wouse's appearance is so bizarre and distorted that it lacks a human model. Like Slipslop's, the landlady's portrait is emblematic, suggesting her likeness to a weasel. Every special feature of that animal, including its long brown, is alluded to in her portrait: she has a short, thin body, a crooked back, a projecting forehead and a small head with tiny, red eyes. Like da Vinci in his *Portrait of a Lady with an Ermine*, Fielding compares his subject to an auxiliary object—in both cases an animal. And although Mrs. Tow-wouse is not literally carnivorous, her treatment of her husband and her indigent guests mark her as the most ferocious, bloodthirsty, weasel-like figure in the novel.

Fielding's Reynolds-like portraits of Fanny and Joseph are admirable for their methodical description and full detail, which is not true of the portraits of such people as Didapper, Trulliber, and Mrs. Tow-wouse, and yet the latter are vivid and memorable sketches. Coleridge, speaking of Wordsworth's poetic faults, provides a clue to this effectiveness in his shrewd appreciation of these two methods of "painting." Of the full description he says:

> Such descriptions too often occasion in the mind of a reader, who is determined to understand his author, a feeling of labor, not very dissimilar to that, with which he would construct a diagram, line by line, for a long geometrical proposition. It seems to be like taking the pieces of a dissected map out of its box. We first look at one part, and then at another, then join and dove-tail them; and when the successive acts of attention have been completed, there is a retrogressive effort of mind to behold it as a whole.[27]

Although Coleridge saw certain values in this method of representation, he would have the poet "paint to the imagination, not to the fancy," and so he prefers description which presents a "co-presence of the whole picture flash'd at once upon the eye, as the sun paints in a camera obscura."[28] To be successful, then, a multitude of images must be reduced and unified in a psychological, not a mechanical, way. It is this economic, unified employment of relevant, visual detail, as well as the bizarre content of these portraits, that makes them some of the most effective in *Joseph Andrews*.

IV

At the beginning of this chapter it was said there is little that is surprising or new in Fielding's character drawing in his second work of prose fiction vis-à-vis his first, and we are now in a position to examine that statement critically. In general, Fielding employed the same formalized devices of characterization in *Joseph Andrews* that he used earlier in *Jonathan Wild*. The manner in which he employed them, however, had changed, and it is here that the development of Fielding's character writing is best revealed. Thus the novelist opens *Joseph Andrews* with the same rhetorical formula with which he presented his hero in *Jonathan Wild;* however, he uses it for only part of the second chapter, and he makes the formula and the assumptions behind it part of the comedy of the novel. "But suppose for Argument's sake," he says, breaking off in the middle of the biographical sketch,

> we should admit that he had no Ancestors at all, but had sprung up, according to the modern Phrase, out of a Dunghill, as the *Athenians* pretended they themselves did from the Earth, would not this *Autokopros* have been justly entitled to all the Praise arising from his own Virtues? Would it not be hard, that a Man who hath no Ancestors should therefore be render'd incapable of acquiring Honour, when we see so many who have no Virtues, enjoying the Honour of their Forefathers?

He can now discard, interrupt, or use for his own special ends techniques he had previously accepted literally, as this pointed and timeless attack on inherited privilege demonstrates.

The same is true of his use of significant names. Although such names are used extensively in *Joseph Andrews*, they are employed with much more subtlety and sophistication than previously. In fact, the major characters, Joseph and Adams, seem to have common names, although it is only gradually that we realize their important biblical resonance. The minor characters' names are more transparent, but even here there is a pleasing indirection in names like Trulliber, Tow-wouse, and Didapper. *Joseph Andrews* makes use of the direct character sketch, but not to the same extent as *Jonathan Wild*.

Two methods of depiction not found in Fielding's first work, idealized portraiture and emblematic description, perform some of the functions of the direct sketch and substantially contribute to the liveliness and variety of the characterization in *Joseph Andrews*. In all these latter portraits and sketches the writer's tone has changed from the caustic irony of *Jonathan Wild* to a robust and iconoclastic comedy that touches even the hero and his reverend mentor. While Fielding still relies on traditional methods to depict character, he uses them with growing originality and spontaneity to increase his control over his material, so that we can expect this tendency to continue and accelerate in *Tom Jones*.

The characters themselves, in the larger context of the total novel, seem to reflect these changes. Most of the figures in *Joseph Andrews* are semiallegorical, they embody individual moral qualities and have some human or psychological dimensions as well. They no longer represent epic vices, like "greatness"; now they are concerned with what Fielding describes as affectations: "The Vices to be found here, are rather the accidental Consequences of some human Frailty, or Foible, than Causes habitually existing in the Mind. . . . they are never the principal Figure . . . on the Scene" (preface).

In general, Fielding's ethical system is still a profound part of *Joseph Andrews*, but it is much less obvious than it was in *Jonathan Wild*. Thus, although most of the characters are still created from the writer's ethical beliefs, not all of them are embodiments of plain vices or virtues. The novel also has a few prominent social types (Didapper, Lady Booby) and humor characters (Adams, Pounce) who have moral dimensions. The more subtle workings of Fielding's ethical system may be observed in the way they relate to each other. These relationships are not based on fine ideological distinctions and hierarchies; broad moral contrasts and antitheses are important to the work, but they are reinforced by psychological and physical affinities.

The predictable conclusions about Fielding's use of established literary forms in his first works of prose fiction suggest that his statement about his new species of writing must be understood in a special sense. In creating *Joseph Andrews* he quite justly conceived of himself as an innovator, yet the origins of much of his prose fiction are clearly rooted in the past, and what this statement means —especially for his character drawing—is that, having conceived of a type of writing not hitherto attempted, Fielding looked backward to the literature of previous ages for the means to realize his unique purposes. He used his experience with drama to great advantage, of course, but he reached boldly beyond it to classical and Renaissance literature. He borrowed from established genres, at first timidly and literally, and experimented in *Jonathan Wild*. He continued to borrow after this, but he adapted, modified, and innovated with increasing imagination and independence, so that by the time he wrote *Joseph Andrews* the signs of borrowing are difficult to detect.

It is also evident that what has been said thus far about the ethical nature of Fielding's characterizations bears on his moral purpose and tone in his early works. Despite the scholarship of people like Cross and Work, many critics seem unconvinced of the importance of his ethical system for his novels, and particularly for *Tom Jones*. Their misapprehension should be clear from what has already been said on this subject. If scrutiny of Fielding's characters reveals anything, it is that—from the time of his earliest work of prose fiction—the novelist's point of view was always profoundly ethical. Indeed, it is not an exaggeration to say that Fielding's aesthetic imagination cannot be separated from his moral vision. And *Tom Jones* is further testimony to such an analysis.

CHAPTER FOUR

---•◆•---

Tom Jones

(T)HE RANGE of Fielding's characterization has generated more critical interest in *Tom Jones* than in any of his other works of prose fiction. Discussion of its nature and merits is filled with disagreement and contradiction. For example, one critic sees the figures as belonging to functionally defined classes that are largely concerned with embodying the author's aesthetic standards and moral intentions.[1] Another scholar's judgment is quite different; analyzing the characters *en masse* he maintains: "The personages in *Tom Jones* are as real and life-like as any in literature." For him, "realistic portraiture" is the "glory of this book pre-eminently."[2] A third scholar's opinion is different still: "The characters themselves are not, in the fullest sense, people. They are almost all 'flat' characters in the tradition of the comedy of humours. . . . The point, here, is not that the 'humours' tradition is invalid but that it does not quite square with the larger claims of Fielding to present a true and realistic picture of 'human nature.' "[3]

This chapter, because of its specialized interest, does not pretend to arbitrate the critical disagreement about all aspects of Fielding's characterization in *Tom Jones*.

It suggests, however, that there seems to be an important relationship between these disagreements and the different form of direct literary portraiture in *Tom Jones* vis-à-vis *Jonathan Wild* and *Joseph Andrews*.

I

Like Fielding's previous major works of prose fiction, *Tom Jones* begins with a character sketch, "A short Description of Squire Allworthy." First this pivotal figure and then an artfully chosen panorama of characters in his circle are introduced: the village folk, the neighboring squire (with his sister and daughter), and a miscellaneous company of doctors, parsons, lawyers, and city people.[4] We shall examine these figures according to the conventional neoclassic patterns of contrast and antithesis in which Fielding arranged them to realize his traditional moral purposes in this novel.

Its moral center as well as its social hub, Allworthy is the person of greatest moral stature and integrity in the book. All questions of legal and personal guilt and innocence are referred to him for arbitration (Jenny, Partridge, Black George, Tom). He is the allegorical yardstick that others (Blifil, Western, Tom) are explicitly or implicitly compared to. As the ethical touchstone of the novel, it is appropriate that his character be presented at the outset as a reference point for every character that will follow him.

Squire Allworthy is introduced in a sketch that combines, in a somewhat elevated style, narrative and psychological description.

In that part of the western division of this kingdom, which is commonly called Somersetshire, there lately lived (and perhaps lives still) a gentleman whose name was Allworthy, and who might well be called the favourite of both Nature and Fortune; for both of these seem to have contended which should bless and enrich him most. In this contention, Nature may seem to some to have come off victorious, as she bestowed on him many gifts; while Fortune had only one gift in her power; but in pouring forth this, she was so very profuse, that others perhaps may think this single endowment to have been more than equivalent to all the various blessings which he enjoyed from Nature. From the former of these, he derived an agreeable person, a sound constitution, a solid understanding, and a benevolent heart; by the latter, he was decreed to the inheritance of one of the largest estates in the county. (Bk. 1, ch. 2)

The most striking aspects of this miniature biographical sketch are its abstractness and simplicity. Indeed, the use of only one specific detail (the reference to Somersetshire as Allworthy's home) seems calculated to introduce a figure whose character is purposefully cerebral. The focus of the description is the squire's benevolence, which is first suggested in an indirect fashion and then is communicated directly in the climactic sentences of the sketch. However, the eighteenth-century idea of benevolence which Allworthy embodies (he is a personified abstraction of good nature and not an abstract character who is benevolent) was quite complex, and it implied a social affection that involved the individual sympathetically and selflessly in the affairs of humanity.[5] Fielding himself described it as an "amiable temper of mind, which disposes us to feel the misfortunes, and enjoy the happiness of others; and, consequently, pushes us on to promote the latter, and prevent the former; and that without any abstract contemplation on the beauty of virtue, and without the allurements or terrors of religion" (14: 285). There could be no more apt epitome of Allworthy's character, or the moral life-pattern the novel seeks to promote, than is contained in this definition.

Two other significant qualities are mentioned. Though it is not described, we are told that the squire has "an agreeable person," which is an important symbolic characteristic because it is a manifestation of a nature that is equally without blemish. The squire is also endowed with a "solid understanding," which, like Parson Adams's "good sense," does not play a significant part in the way the former is realized in the action of the novel.

This view of his character, as an allegorization of benevolence, is confirmed by Allworthy's name. Without a Christian name to particularize him, "All-worthy" is one of the few characters in *Tom Jones* whose surname is overtly significant. The reaction to this name by a Frenchman writing in the *Gentleman's Magazine* in March 1750 indicates how Fielding's contemporaries understood the character and how favorably they reacted to it: "The name of *Allworthy*, which in *English* signifies *supereminently good*, could never be more justly bestow'd than on the respectable uncle of *Jones*."[6] Though Fielding's brief passage (above) constitutes all of Allworthy's introductory description, it does not include all the direct analysis of the squire's character. At least three times in the novel, in smaller, less methodized descriptions, the notion of Allworthy's basic benevolence is repeated. On one occasion, for example, he is called "a human being replete with benevolence" (bk. 1, ch. 4), and on another we are told that "cruelty and injustice were two ideas, of which Mr Allworthy could by no means support the consciousness a single moment" (bk. 3, ch. 2). These one-line psychological sketches serve two purposes: they justify actions about to be attributed to Allworthy and they keep this cardinal virtue (which is one of the central concerns of the novel) before our eyes.

As in Thomas Heartfree's and Parson Adams's depictions, details of physical appearance are not supplied for Squire Allworthy, as they are for people like Joseph and Tom, and the absence of explicit descriptions suggests the roles they play. Embodying the book's highest standards of ethical conduct, they are archetypes of human goodness or benevolence, and all, in varying degree, are morally superhuman figures. Appropriately, Fielding did not choose to depict in detailed or elaborately visual terms characters who play such abstract, allegorical, or near allegorical roles.[7] In general, the novelist's idealizing and caricaturing depictions are related to the high degree of emotional identification or rejection he expects toward certain characters (his heroes, heroines, and minor villains are described by such visual modes), and the figures for whom he expects more detached, intellectualized responses are depicted less elaborately.

Because Allworthy is not a rounded figure, he has been condemned by a number of twentieth-century critics. George Sherburn dismisses him as "a mere formula, not a live person."[8] André Gide called him "a dubious creation."[9] F. Holmes Dudden's opinion probably best represents the prevailing critical estimate: "In this personage the novelist aimed at picturing an ideally good man. Unfortunately he attempted to do this by means of presenting a glorified portrait of his friend and patron, Ralph Allen of Bath. The result is not successful. . . . But whatever the reason of the failure may have been, the figure of Allworthy is stiff, and wooden, and lacking in lifelikeness—though R. L. Stevenson somewhat exaggerated when he described it as 'only ink and paper.' "[10]

Dudden, and those who agree with him, are partially right; there is something stiff and uncomfortably "episcopal" about Allworthy that makes him seem flat and allegorical.[11] The problem, however, is that Fielding *intended* that he should be flat and allegorical because of his ethical function. Thus critics who condemn Allworthy seem to do so because of a preoccupation with the flat-round type of character analysis that blinds them to the uses of Fielding's allegorization. Even critics who are unusually sensitive to the novelist's modes of character depiction stray a bit in their evaluation of Allworthy. The implication of Sheldon Sacks's comparison of Adams, Allworthy, and Harrison frequently seems to be that Allworthy is the least vital of these three paragons.[12] Such a conclusion is surely of limited validity because of the differences among the three novels and—more particularly—because Adams and Harrison are major characters whereas Allworthy is a minor figure.

Tom Jones depends for much of its vivid characterization on many of the same kinds of antithesis we have seen in the writer's previous novels. In this novel, as in *Jonathan Wild* and *Joseph Andrews*, Fielding employs antithesis as a vehicle for his ethical system, although this device also has aesthetic appeal as well as rhetorical function, serving to set the characters off against one another with force and clarity. Joseph Trapp expresses the principle: "Contraries illustrate, and recommend each other by Comparison. . . . When the thoughts are thus set against each other, they appear with Energy, and strike the Mind with redoubled Force."[13] Moreover, the artificial quality of this contrast contributes to the comic distance that is necessary for the proper remove between the novel's reader and its characters. Again, the antithetical arrangement helps define the moral boundaries of the questions considered, and while it invites detachment from the characters, it compels judgment and evaluation of them and the points of view they represent.[14]

One of the best examples of this kind of antithesis as a method of characterization is the presentation of Squires Allworthy and Western, who are intended to establish a multilevel contrast: the man of reason versus the man of impulse, the man of culture versus the boor, the man of learning versus the man of ignorance. Such antitheses are also important means of providing a perspective that reinforces the comedy in much of Western's actions. By means of one character we see the worth of the other; the values and actions of each are defined and clarified by means of the ironic contrast that both, together, create.

Western is not directly characterized in *Tom Jones*. He is not an absolute villain but, like Falstaff, an elemental person, anterior to right and wrong, and so is not depicted by the highly visual portrait usually reserved for the minor figures that represent vices or affectations important in Fielding's ethical thought.[15] The novelist had created several prototypes of Western in his dramas (Sir Positive Trap in *Love in Several Masques*, Squire Badger in *Don Quixote in England*, Sir Harry Foxchase and Squire Tankard in *The Election*),[16] and he seems to have drawn on his work with these figures in presenting Western through exclusively dramatic techniques.

Western is not the only figure who contrasts with Allworthy. In the definition of benevolence cited above (from Fielding's "Essay on the Knowledge of the Characters of Men") to illuminate Allworthy's character, the novelist mentions three distinct sources of virtuous action: (1) sympathy, (2) philosophic love of virtue, and (3) the inducements of religion. The apparently antithetic motives of religion and virtue are judged spurious for several reasons, which are implicit here and throughout Fielding's writings. The abstract, philosophic love of virtue is rejected because he believed that virtues of the mind—indeed almost all cerebral motives—are amoral in tendency if not in nature. The allure and terror of religion are rejected for the simple reason that Fielding believed they are weak and insufficient motivating forces. Because of their suspect nature, then, these sources or motives are closely associated with the rhetoric of hypocrisy. In the context of Fielding's "Essay on the Knowledge of the Characters of Men," which deals primarily with the deviousness of hypocrisy, it is clear that "contemplation on the beauty of virtue" and the "allurements or terrors of religion" are high-sounding but hollow, pretentious phrases that hypocrites use to cloak their self-centered purposes. Only "sympathy," Fielding maintains, is the true fountainhead of benevolence.

Employing his compressed definition of good nature as a guide, Fielding used its three parts as the pattern for separate characters in his novel. From his conception of benevolence spring the three figures whom he advances as teachers and guides: Thwackum, Square, and Allworthy. Each figure is a dramatization or incarnation of one of the motives outlined above, and their functions and interrelationships, as well as their origin, are derived from this important definition. Together, these three figures illustrate Fielding's statement, exemplifying its implications and dramatizing its truth. Acting in close concert,

they demonstrate the shallowness, insufficiency, and—
most important of all—hypocritical tendency of weak
religious and philosophic motives or professions. At the
same time they reveal, by the pointed contrast they create, the strength and vitality of unsophisticated human
sympathy as a wellspring of virtuous action.

Thomas Square is Fielding's objectification of his belief
in the insufficiency of the contemplation and love of
virtue as a basis for benevolent action. The initial description of Square as a very broad type-character prepares the
reader for his later appearance as a representative or allegorical figure; he is not introduced by a proper name but
by the generic designation "the Philosopher." The earliest
clue to Square's nature is the statement that he "formed
his morals on the Platonic model." In "An Essay on Conversation," published in Fielding's *Miscellanies*, he characterized Plato as reasoning "on the native beauty of
virtue" (14: 267) and thereby identified Plato with this
catch phrase, which is also found in the novelist's definition of good nature. That Square, a professed disciple of
Plato in matters of virtue, verbally subscribes to this Platonic ideal is incontrovertible, but Fielding does not leave
the connection between Square's ethos and its source so
tenuous. Instead, he characterizes Square by a cant phrase,
"the natural beauty of virtue"—his "favourite phrase,"
which is so similar to the phrase from his definition of
benevolence ("without any abstract contemplation on
the beauty of virtue") that it confirms the fact that he
intended Square to be an embodiment of a moral position
which he, Fielding, rejects.

The nonsense rhetoric of "the Philosopher" in such
phrases as "the *unalterable rule of right*, and the *eternal
fitness of things*" (bk. 3, ch. 3) and "quadrate with the

unerring rule of right" (bk. 4, ch. 11) serves, like Square's name, to identify the pseudo-scientific and mathematically inclined deists of the eighteenth century with Square, while it also ridicules the comic absurdity of their position. After Fielding establishes Square's character by means of this set-piece description, he employs his conduct to expose the reality behind the high-sounding clichés he represents. Egotistical and self-centered, Square illustrates the jejune nature of his "virtues." For this reason he is a comic figure, exposed by his petty, selfish conduct and his vacuous moral pretensions.

Thwackum's character is established and developed as an allegorization of "the allurements or terrors of religion," the second part of Fielding's antithesis in his definition of benevolence. From the time of Thwackum's introduction, where he is called "the Divine," his ethos is defined in terms of religion, and his conduct and rhetoric flow directly from his "religious" character. His name alerts us to his devotion to punishment and terror: his meditations, both on the natural and the supernatural, "were full of birch" (bk. 3, ch. 5). "Had not my hand been with-held from due correction," he says of his harsh treatment of Tom, "I had scourged much of this diabolical spirit out of a boy, of whom from his infancy I discovered the devil had taken such entire possession" (bk. 18, ch. 4). Although Thwackum's character is most closely associated with corporal punishment, he invokes the terrors of eternal punishment with equal facility. For example, he tells Allworthy, in a tone more ominous and threatening than optimistic, that he hopes Tom "may not seal up his final commitment to the place of wailing and gnashing of teeth" (ibid.).

While Thwackum's conduct speaks most forcefully

of his belief in terror, his rhetoric alleges his devotion to grace, the most winning of religion's allurements. His favorite phrase is "the *divine power of grace*" (bk. 3, ch. 3). He believes man is a sink of iniquity, capable of being redeemed only by religion's (the Church of England's) power. Outside the fold of grace, Thwackum preaches, there is only eternal damnation.

Between these two false teachers, both of whom have "discarded all natural goodness of heart" (bk. 3, ch. 4), stands the novel's only true guide, Squire Allworthy, who combines and practices the virtues which Thwackum and Square merely profess. "His mind," Fielding tells us, "was, indeed, tempered with that philosophy which becomes a man and a Christian" (bk. 6, ch. 3). Reflecting on the relationship between Thwackum, Square, and himself, Allworthy even pictures himself as a mean between two extremes. "He thought indeed that the different exuberancies of these gentlemen, would correct their different imperfections; and that from both, especially with his assistance, the two lads would derive sufficient precepts of true religion and virtue" (bk. 3, ch. 5). The squire, then, is Fielding's principal realization of his prefatory commitment "to recommend goodness and innocence," Allworthy's outstanding virtues, by giving the reader "a kind of picture, in which virtue becomes as it were an object of sight, and strikes us with an idea of that loveliness, which Plato asserts there is in her naked charms" (*Tom Jones*, dedication).[17]

That these three figures are primarily allegorical characters associated with Fielding's three-part analysis of benevolence in his "Essay on the Knowledge of the Characters of Men" is borne out by the fact that they are consistently identified by concepts that connect them to the appropriate parts of the definition. Thwackum and Square, referred to throughout as "the Divine" and "the Philosopher," are identified with the words "religion" and "virtue." Commenting on his purpose in creating Thwackum and Square, Fielding points to what these figures represent when he says that he did not draw them to "give offence to any, especially to men who are warm in the cause of virtue or religion." On the contrary, "it is with a view to their service [religion's and virtue's] that I have taken upon me to record the lives and actions of two of their false and pretended champions. A treacherous friend is the most dangerous enemy; and I will say boldly, that both religion and virtue have received more real discredit from hypocrites, than the wittiest profligates or infidels could ever cast upon them" (bk. 3, ch. 4).

On the other hand, Allworthy, whose benevolence and open heart the narrator lauds insistently, is called "a pattern" of goodness (bk. 6, ch. 3). In his dictionary, Samuel Johnson best explains what Fielding meant by "pattern" when he defined the word as "the original proposed to imitation; the archetype; that which is to be copied; an exemplar."[18]

The technique of identifying these three figures with single concepts,[19] their lack of particularizing physical description, and their simple, pointed character analyses are not aimed at individualizing but at maintaining them at their uniquely representative status as intellectual ciphers. This is true in a special way of Thwackum and Square, of course. Not only are they lacking in individuality, they are pointedly grotesque and artificial because they are objects of derision and negative models. Allworthy, on the other hand, is a more pleasant type than either of his acquaintances because he is less an ideological caricature.

The close moral interaction among these figures and the carefully contrived contrast by which they are presented in *Tom Jones* confirm this analysis. The overwhelming majority of Fielding's characters appear in pairs in a simple good-bad contrast or antithesis. Using the pattern common in English character books and generally associated with Christian ethics, the novelist contrasts the villainous Blifil with the good Jones, the benevolent Heartfree with the wicked Wild, the good-hearted Adams with the selfish Trulliber. In drawing Allworthy, Thwackum, and Square, however, he resorted to the method of contrast used by Theophrastus and based on Aristotelian ethics, which views virtue as a *via media* between two extremes. Thus Allworthy, his virtue and religiosity combined in his own good nature, exemplifies a middle way between the false extremes of the abstract philosopher and the hollow divine—a pattern that accounts for their predictable behavior in the plot. When all three figures appear together, a moral question is raised, whereupon Square gives his solution, Thwackum offers his equally erroneous (and equally predictable) view, and Allworthy settles the matter by rejecting both men's statements and providing the true solution, based on true benevolence.

Although Thwackum and Square are corrupt, they are not equally villainous; Fielding seems to draw Square much less harshly than he portrays Thwackum. The philosopher is never so violent, cruel, or sadistic as the divine. Considerably humanized and subdued by being discovered in Molly's bedroom, Square falls sick shortly after this, and when he is confronted with death his empty philosophy is in effect renounced and he dies a good Christian. And again, the key to this difference in portrayal seems to be in Fielding's "Essay on the Knowledge of the Characters of Men," much of which is an analysis of two different types of hypocrisy. The lowest species of this vice, and the one Fielding paints with greatest fury, is "censoriousness"—which, as Henry Knight Miller points out, bears upon many of the novelist's character portraits.[20] But this censoriousness throws more light on Thwackum's nature than on any other figure in Fielding's novels. Declaring against the sanctified hypocrisy that resides only in the countenance and on the lips, Fielding immediately gets to the heart of Thwackum's character.

> A sour, morose, ill-natured, censorious sanctity, never is, nor can be sincere. Is a readiness to despise, to hate, and to condemn, the temper of a Christian? Can he, who passes sentence on the souls of men with more delight and triumph than the devil can execute it, have the impudence to pretend himself a disciple of One who dies for the sins of mankind?[21]

Not content with even this bitter denunciation, Fielding continues with his analysis and condemnation.

> As this is a most detestable character in society; and as its malignity is more particularly bent against the best and worthiest men, the sincere and open-hearted, whom it persecutes with inveterate envy and hatred, I shall take some pains in the ripping it up. . . .
> [A]s it will do nothing honestly to deserve reputation, so is it ever industrious to deprive others of the praises due to their virtues. It confines all merit to those

external forms which are fully particularised in Scripture; of these it is itself a rigid observer. . . .

[D]oth it not attempt to cheat men into the pursuit of sorrow and misery, under the appearance of virtue, and to frighten them from mirth and pleasure under the colour of vice, or, if you please, sin? (14:294–98)

It is clear from all this that Thwackum, in Fielding's eyes, is a genuine villain, for he not only distorts and perverts the Christian religion but attacks those who practice its commandments. It would be difficult to conceive of a more heinous Fielding character.

Like Allworthy, Thwackum and Square are usually regarded as insubstantial, flat creations. Both have recently been described as playing parts "to which the ethical beliefs Fielding imposes on them are quite irrelevant."[22] This, however, is not the case; their conception and functions in the novel are more a matter of careful thought and integration than the reader may suppose. Linked together inseparably, all three characters operate as an integral part of Fielding's attempt to define benevolence in *Tom Jones*. Intended as intellectual ciphers, they are lively and effective examples of their kind. In the world of the novel, their flatness and allegorical natures are the very qualities by which the intellectual and ethical positions they personify can be examined and judged.

While the Thwackum-Square antithesis is most carefully devised and executed, it is not the most important one; the central antithesis is between Tom and Blifil. Allworthy is the paragon of the novel, representing a degree of virtue utterly unattainable. Tom is a realistic human mean, between Allworthy's virtue and Western's boisterous amorality, and he develops in character from a status close to Western's at the beginning of the novel to an approximation of Allworthy's at the very end.[23] Throughout, Tom represents Fielding's conception of an average "good man"—the credibly human picture of a benevolence that is eminently attainable. He is the key figure in the novel in the sense that he is the character who will influence and appeal to most readers. Consequently, Fielding takes great pains to draw him effectively. He sets Tom side by side with Blifil and, as with Wild and Heartfree, makes both of them as identical in background and situation as possible. In this juxtaposition, both are instructively schematic figures, each with his own function. Tom is meant to reveal the true nature of human goodness. Negatively and less importantly (for the emphasis in *Tom Jones* is always positive, in contrast to *Jonathan Wild*), Blifil exposes the nature of hypocrisy.

Blifil has less direct characterization than Tom; he is portrayed on a number of occasions but always briefly, and when he is described it is for the purpose of comparing him to Tom. Treated in much the same way as Heartfree in *Jonathan Wild*, Blifil is not depicted in an independent, formal character sketch, while Tom is usually characterized as an entity apart from his half brother. These facts, all pointing to Blifil's function, partly explain the reason for the circumscribed dimensions of his character.

The first passage in which Blifil is described sets the pattern for those that follow.

The vices of this young man [Jones] were, moreover, heightened, by the disadvantageous light in which they appeared, when opposed to the virtues of Master Blifil, his companion: a youth of so different a cast from little Jones, that not only the family, but all the neighborhood, resounded his praises. He was, indeed, a lad of a remarkable disposition; sober, discreet, and pious, beyond his age. (Bk. 3, ch. 2)

This brief, comparative sketch of psychological characterization is of very limited function: it sets up a transparently false contrast (Tom is presented as villain and Blifil as hero) that the judgment of the plot will examine and explicitly reverse. There is more concern on the author's part with the ironic tone of this passage than with the character of Blifil. In contrast to Tom's presentation, no details are given about Blifil's appearance; because of his abstract function, he exists without physical reality, as an unembodied, intellectual antithesis. Blifil's qualities are chosen for their contrast to the open, unsophisticated disposition of Tom. However, these qualities do not condemn Blifil as an outright villian (although a degree of hypocrisy is implied in "pious, beyond his age"); they merely present him as an unlikely paragon of unappealing virtues.

It is in the later, formal characterizations and in the spiteful acts of cruelty and deception (functions of his antithetical purpose) that his villainous character is established, that he is exposed as a duplicitous figure masquerading behind a façade of conventional respectability. Two passages in particular are responsible for this change. The first of these again contrasts Tom and Blifil, but this time to the undisguised discredit of the latter.

As there are some minds whose affections, like Master Blifil's, are solely placed on one single person, whose interest and indulgence alone they consider on every occasion; regarding the good and ill of all others as merely indifferent . . . so there is a different temper of mind which borrows a degree of virtue even from self-love; such can never receive any kind of satisfaction from another, without loving the creature to whom that satisfaction is owing, and without making its well-being in some sort necessary to their own ease. Of this latter species was our heroe. (Bk. 4, ch. 6)

The second passage, the only one in which a direct contrast with Tom is merely implicit, is an outright attack and condemnation of Blifil rather than a description of his nature.

His appetites were, by nature, so moderate, that he was easily able, by philosophy or by study, or by some other method, to subdue them; and as to that passion which we have treated of in the first chapter of this book, he had not the least tincture of it in his whole composition.

But tho' he was so entirely free from that mixed passion, of which we there treated, and of which the virtues and beauty of Sophia formed so notable an object; yet was he altogether as well furnished with some other passions, that promised themselves very full gratification in the young lady's fortune. Such were avarice and ambition, which divided the dominion of his mind between them. (Bk. 6, ch. 4)

The degree to which Blifil's character is merely a reversal of Tom's becomes very clear in this final English character sketch. Sexual moderation, implicitly condemned in Blifil, becomes sexual license in Tom and is countenanced as natural; avarice becomes generosity and ambition becomes unpretentious selflessness. Both his vice-like character and its relatively few components define Blifil as a semiallegorical figure who stands somewhere between his mentors, Thwackum and Square, who are personifications of a single quality, and such complex, fully developed type characters as Tom.

Blifil's character is one of the least successful in the novel; he does not come off as human nor is he entirely successful as an intellectual cartoon. There is very little development of his character; he is not given a first name; and his allegorical nature is drawn without much energy or power. Presented as Tom's antithesis, his character is not so complexly developed as the hero's, and as a result he is a rather weak foil. Finally, while Blifil is a semi-allegorical figure, Tom, his antithesis, is the most human figure in the novel, and in a contrast of this kind Blifil must inevitably pale. Even the overzealous efforts of scholars to publish "identifications" of the novel's characters have not produced, or even hinted at, a live model for Blifil. It would indeed be difficult to advance stronger testimony to this character's complete unreality.

Tom's characterization, significantly, is more complex. To begin with, there is no formal description of his ethos at his introduction as there is with Blifil. His name, a compound of the two most common names in England, seems to label him an unheroic, average male.[24] Except for this nominal distinction, Fielding presents Tom through his speech and actions in the first quarter of the book, and later there are several minor passages of direct psychological description. In the middle of the novel, a lengthy and elaborate physical and psychological account of Tom is provided, and this is followed by several brief, casual descriptions in the last half of the novel.

For the most part, these passages of psychological characterization are slight matters, merely complementing the tone of the scenes or justifying actions about to be performed. "Jones had naturally violent animal spirits," we are told, and at once we are shown these spirits, heated by the effects of wine. Or is it proclaimed that "Jones, who, notwithstanding his good humour, had some mixture of the irascible," and directly his irascibility is displayed. Two of these short, formal characterizations, however, are somewhat more involved. The first occurs when Tom is examined by the officer who is leading a company against the pretender. "For, besides that he [Tom] was very well dressed, and was naturally genteel, he had a remarkable air of dignity in his look, which it is rarely seen among the vulgar, and is indeed not inseparably annexed to the features of their superiors" (bk. 7, ch. 11). As description, this is rather abstract, but what it loses in visual richness it gains in subtle elevation. Such phrases as "a remarkable air of dignity . . . rarely seen among the vulgar" alert the reader to the fact that Tom is not a common bastard.

The same point is made more forcefully and explicitly in the next description, a detailed passage that occurs when Tom rescues Mrs. Waters from the villain Northerton. "Indeed he was a charming figure, and if a very fine person, and a most comely set of features, adorned with youth, health, strength, freshness, spirit, and good nature, can make a man resemble an angel, he certainly had that resemblance" (bk. 9, ch. 2). Again, Tom's distinguished appearance and aristocratic air are stressed by the flattering, generalized description, whose emphasis is on his positive qualities, and particularly his physical appearance. There is a knightly quality to this description of Mrs. Waters's savior:[25] he is charming, comely, youthful, strong, spirited, and angelic—qualities long established as those of the knightly hero in romance.[26] And the choice of these qualities has another ramification: all of these attributes have calculated sexual overtones that help explain Tom's powerful effect on the lady he rescues.

Many of the same points are also made in the novel's principal description of Jones. Indeed, his full-length portrait is an almost lyrical summary or orchestration of his earlier physical, psychological, and dramatic depictions. Part of the amorous dinner scene between Mrs. Waters and Tom in the inn at Upton, this portrait sketches both his agreeable, good-natured disposition and his overwhelming attractiveness.

> Mr Jones . . . was in reality, one of the handsomest young fellows in the world. His face, besides being the picture of health, had in it the most apparent marks of sweetness and good-nature. These qualities were indeed so characteristical in his countenance, that while the spirit and sensibility in his eyes, tho' they must have been perceived by an accurate observer, might have escaped the notice of the less discerning, so strongly was this good-nature painted in his look, that it was remarked by almost everyone who saw him.
>
> It was, perhaps, as much owing to this, as to a very fine complection, that his face had a delicacy in it almost inexpressible, and which might have given him an air rather too effeminate, had it not been joined to a most masculine person and mien; which latter had as much in them of the Hercules, as the former had of the Adonis. He was besides active, genteel, gay, and good-humoured, and had a flow of animal spirits, which enlivened every conversation where he was present. (Bk. 9, ch. 5)

The primary point of this portrait is the idealized beauty of the hero, presented by means of the novelist's standard anatomical catalogue but in a more abbreviated form than usual. It is also clear that Fielding is employing the tradition of idealized description that was used to portray nobility, who were often knights or chivalric figures. This sketch presents Tom (whose "heroic disposition" prompts him to become a soldier at one point in his career) in terms similar to those employed in the common portrait of the knight in the works of writers like Scudéry. The similarities between Tom and the typical knight from *Almahide* suggest not that Tom's portrait was based on this particular sketch but that it is in the same mold as the knightly Abindarrays.

> His Stature, as you know is of the middle size, between too big and too little: but so fine, so noble, and so pliant, that there is nothing more to be desired. He hath an high Air, a majestick Port, a sober Gate, and an Action a little fierce: but all this temper'd, however, with so much sweetness, that it causes him as much amity, as the other qualities give him respect and esteem. His Hair which is not too black nor too light, is of a very pleasant colour, his visage is oval, and just and proportionable in every part: His Eyes are black, large and well open'd, but wholly full of Spirit and Love: His Eye-brows brown and very thick, his Complexion lively, his Nose well made, though somewhat big for a *Granadine;* and his Mouth so extraordinary fine, both for shape and colour, that the fairest Lady would be content to have such a one: and then when he smiles, it stretches it self so pleasantly with his Visage, that it is the most lovely sight that Eyes ever beheld: He hath also the finest hands in the World for a man.[27]

The numerous close similarities between Tom and Abindarrays could hardly have been missed by the readers for whom Fielding intended *Tom Jones*. Both characters have the same imposing air, perfect masculine build, lively countenance, fine complexion, sweet yet masculine mien, eyes of spirit and love—or sensibility—and just a hint of effeminacy. Fielding puts all this to several uses in an association which sits better with the gallant Jones than, in similar but less emphatic innuendo, with the virtuous Joseph Andrews. It provides context for the relationship between Tom and Mrs. Waters. Described just before we are told that Mrs. Waters is "in love" with him, Tom's appearance has even more emphatic sexual overtones than in his previous description. His body is compared to Hercules, a symbol of masculine power and strength, and his face is likened to that of Adonis, the companion of the goddess of love and the epitome of male attractiveness. Besides such physical charm, Tom has a warm disposition and generous animal spirits, which helps put the case for his and Mrs. Waters's lapse in middle-class morality very sympathetically.

On the one hand we are again reminded of the hero's open disposition; on the other we are impressed by the powerful, almost mythic attraction of his appearance on the women he encounters and their equally strong effect on him. While these two considerations may not, in some minds, exculpate either character, Fielding intended them to be taken into account in any judgment of their conduct, but especially in a judgment of Mrs. Waters, whom the novelist realized is the more vulnerable. "When the reader hath duly reflected on these many charms which all centered in our heroe, and considers at the same time the fresh obligations which Mrs Waters had to him," he remarks at the conclusion of Tom's sketch, "it will be a mark of more prudery than candour to entertain a bad opinion of her, because she conceived a very good opinion of him" (bk. 9, ch. 5).

Fielding, as we have mentioned, knew that his readers associated this mode of description with the presentation of gentlemen and nobility. And not only does he play on these associations, he strengthens their implications on other occasions. In a previous description, for example, he portrayed Tom as "genteel" and having "a remarkable air of dignity in his look, which it is rarely seen among the vulgar." In a later passage, he speaks of Jones as one who "was better bred than most who frequent it [court]" and as having in a very eminent degree "a certain air of natural gentility, which it is neither in the power of dress to give, nor to conceal." These statements, conveying important information about Tom's nature and circumstances, inescapably imply that Tom is not an ordinary man, that his commonplace name is ironic and is not indicative of his birth or inherent status. Readers who were alert to Fielding's intention would have gone beyond this obvious conclusion to the realization that this description and the calculated mystery surrounding his entrance into the world point to his high birth. The awareness of this fact, however vaguely present in the reader's mind, is something Fielding relies on. The intimation that Tom is high born brings assurance, however tenuous, that he will ultimately receive his due and will be restored to his rightful position. It also gives the reader that sense of security about Tom's fate that Ronald S. Crane shows is one of the bases for the success of the novel.[28]

In his long description we note an almost casual comparison of Tom's masculine form to Adonis, and the same identification is made on another occasion. "Perhaps," Fielding says, "the famed Adonis was not a lovelier figure [than Tom]" (bk. 8, ch. 4). Tom's identification with a mythological figure seems designed to highlight certain aspects of his character—his manly beauty, his love of hunting, his attractiveness to women—but it does much more than merely reinforce different dimensions of his personality. Its full significance is found in the fact that Sophia is identified with Adonis's jealous partner, when, in her portrait, she is compared to Venus and to the statue of the Venus dei Medici.[29] In mythologizing the heroine and hero as Venus and Adonis, Fielding has a subtle comic purpose: in the legend of Adonis, Venus is the aggressive, sophisticated partner; in *Tom Jones*, the same reversal of the traditional male-female relationship occurs, as Tom, with his delicate face and "air rather too effeminate," plays a passive role on a number of occasions. Although Tom does not seem to realize it, Sophia's efforts to win him are far more effective and clever. When he tries—like Adonis—to run off, she chases him; and ultimately, with much more success than Venus, she wins him permanently.

Despite all the detail in this sketch, it is not a sharp visual picture. It lacks the fullness and color of Abindarrays's depiction, and gives us very little idea of what Tom looks like. We know he is good looking, but we have no particulars about his appearance. Minute description was contrary to the century's regard for the principle of decorum, to its emphasis on generality and *la belle nature*,[30] and Tom's idealized appearance is related more to the mood of the events at the inn at Upton than to providing the reader a photographic likeness. But if the portrait lacks a certain visual explicitness, it is not an inept psychological and moral study. A lively English sketch of Tom's dramatic characterization throughout the book, it presents a frank, open person with a good heart, who is no model of human perfection but has qualities of honesty that promise he is open to improvement.

II

The portrait of Sophia is the most complex formal piece of character drawing Fielding ever attempted. An entire chapter long, it employs almost all of his standard techniques of direct characterization in four easily distinguishable parts. The first part is a rhetorically flamboyant exhortation to all nature to celebrate the heroine's appearance in the novel:

> Hushed be every ruder breath. May the heathen ruler of the winds confine in iron chains the boisterous limbs of noisy Boreas, and the sharp-pointed nose of bitter-biting Eurus. Do thou, sweet Zephyrus, rising from thy fragrant bed, mount the western sky, and lead on those delicious gales, the charms of which call forth the lovely Flora from her chamber, perfumed with pearly dews, when on the first of June, her birthday, the blooming maid, in loose attire, gently trips it over the verdant mead, where every flower rises to do her homage, 'till the whole field becomes enamelled, and colours contend with sweets which shall ravish her most.
>
> So charming may she now appear; and you the feather'd choristers of nature, whose sweetest notes not even Handel can excel, tune your melodious throats, to celebrate her appearance. From love proceeds your music, and to love it returns. Awaken therefore that gentle passion in every swain: for lo! adorned with all the charms in which nature can array her; bedecked with beauty, youth, sprightliness, innocence, modesty, and

tenderness, breathing sweetness from her rosy lips, and darting brightness from her sparkling eyes, the lovely Sophia comes.

The second section presents a number of comparisons between the heroine and various works of art:

Reader, perhaps thou hast seen the statue of the *Venus de Medicis*. Perhaps, too, thou hast seen the gallery of beauties at Hampton-Court. Thou may'st remember *each bright* Churchill of the *galaxy*, and all the toasts of the *Kit-cat*. Or if their reign was before thy times, at least thou hast seen their daughters, the no less dazzling beauties of the present age; whose names, should we here insert, we apprehend they would fill the whole volume.

Now if thou hast seen all these, be not afraid of the rude answer which Lord Rochester once gave to a man, who had seen many things. No. If thou hast seen all these without knowing what beauty is, thou hast no eyes; if without feeling its power, thou hast no heart.

Yet it is possible, my friend, that thou mayest have seen all these without being able to form an exact idea of Sophia: for she did not exactly resemble any of them. She was most like the picture of Lady Ranelagh; and I have heard more still to the famous Duchess of Mazarine; but most of all, she resembled one whose image never can depart from my breast, and whom, if thou dost remember, thou hast then, my friend, an adequate idea of Sophia.

In the third part the heroine is described first physically and then psychologically:

Sophia then, the only daughter of Mr Western, was a middle-sized woman; but rather inclining to tall. Her shape was not only exact, but extremely delicate; and the nice proportion of her arms promised the truest symmetry in her limbs. Her hair, which was black, was so luxuriant, that it reached her middle, before she cut it, to comply with the modern fashion; and it was now curled so gracefully in her neck, that few would believe it to be her own. If envy could find any part of her face which demanded less commendation than the rest, it might possibly think her forehead might have been higher without prejudice to her. Her eye-brows were full, even, and arched beyond the power of art to imitate. Her black eyes had a lustre in them, which all her softness could not extinguish. Her nose was exactly regular, and her mouth, in which were two rows of ivory, exactly answered Sir John Suckling's description in those lines.

> Her lips were red, and one was thin
> Compar'd to that was next her chin.
> Some bee had stung it newly.

Her cheeks were of the oval kind; and in her right she had a dimple which the least smile discovered. Her chin had certainly its share in forming the beauty of her face; but it was difficult to say it was either large or small, tho' perhaps it was rather of the former kind. Her complexion had rather more of the lilly than of the rose; but when exercise, or modesty, encreased her natural colour, no vermilion could equal it. Then one might indeed cry out with the celebrated Dr Donne.

> —Her pure and eloquent blood
> Spoke in her cheeks, and so distinctly wrought,
> That one might almost say her body thought.

Her neck was long and finely turned; and here, if I was not afraid of offending her delicacy, I might justly say, the highest beauties of the famous *Venus de Medicis* were outdone. Here was whiteness which no lillies, ivory, nor alabaster could match. The finest cambric

might indeed be supposed from envy to cover that
bosom, which was much whiter than itself,—it was
indeed,

Nitor Splendens Pario marmore purius.
"A gloss shining beyond the purest brightness
of Parian marble."

Such was the outside of Sophia; nor was this beautiful frame disgraced by an inhabitant unworthy of it.
Her mind was every way equal to her person; nay, the
latter borrowed some charms from the former; for
when she smiled, the sweetness of her temper diffused
that glory over her countenance, which no regularity of
features can give. But as there are no perfections of the
mind which do not discover themselves, in that perfect
intimacy, to which we intend to introduce our reader,
with this charming young creature; so it is needless to
mention them here: nay, it is a kind of tacit affront to
our reader's understanding, and may also rob him of that
pleasure which he will receive in forming his own judgment of her character.

The fourth section concludes the portrait with a brief
account of Sophia's education:

It may however, be proper to say, that whatever mental accomplishments she had derived from nature, they
were somewhat improved and cultivated by art: for
she had been educated under the care of an aunt, who
was a lady of great discretion, and was thoroughly acquainted with the world, having lived in her youth
about the Court, whence she had retired some years
since into the country. By her conversation and in-
structions, Sophia was perfectly well bred, though perhaps she wanted a little of that ease in her behaviour,
which is to be acquired only by habit, and living within

what is called the polite circle. But this, to say the truth, is often too dearly purchased; and though it hath charms so inexpressible, that the French, perhaps, among other qualities, mean to express this, when they declare they know not what it is, yet its absence is well compensated by innocence; nor can good sense, and a natural gentility ever stand in need of it.

In the first section, Fielding introduces Sophia in terms of a tableau that has a close pictorial analogue in Guido Reni's *Phoebus and the Hours, Preceded by Aurora*.[31] Reni's works in general, and this picture in particular, were an established part of the neoclassic pantheon, and Fielding certainly knew of them. In Reni's original, Apollo, a picture of youth and beauty, rides in a car that is drawn by wild horses, and he and his procession are the major subject of the work. Aurora, a lovely, blooming figure, flies ahead through a turbulent sky, dropping flowers from both hands and "enamelling" the fields with light and color. Fielding's evocation of this painting retains all the principal subjects but Flora, of course, replaces Aurora and Sophia takes Apollo's place.

There is disagreement about the tone of this tableau and its effect on Sophia, but Fielding himself seems to indicate how it is to be taken in the prefatory chapter in book 4. With obvious irony, he argues that the politician acquires "a good deal of that reverence which attends him through the year, by the several pageants which precede his pomp." His own introduction, he implies, will perform the same function for Sophia. Because of the classical precedent, he will invoke the goddess Flora to assist in this task, and those who object to this heathen deity can think of her as the woman who strews the way with

flowers before processions of noble personages at a cor-
onation. Fielding's attitude toward the function of these
parallel political and dramatic devices indicates that this
passage is to be read ironically.

Although this playful praise is not to be taken literally,
neither was it intended to reflect unfavorably on Sophia,
as various critics have thought.[32] This passage, in the chapter "A short Hint of what we can do in the Sublime," is
really an address in one of the century's most popular
forms, the self-contained mock-epic invocation.[33] A
piece of playful, elaborate rhetoric that is ornamented
with classical literary and visual references, it is cast in
heavily poetic and consciously archaic diction[34] and is a
burlesque of the bombastic introductions and extravagant
descriptions of heroines in romances.[35] This piece serves in
much the same way as the lord mayor's farcical parade:[36]
it is entertainment in its own right (a literary exercise in
the sublime style) and is only indirectly connected with
the description of Sophia. Obviously, Fielding is following a distinction he himself laid down for the prose epic
and is giving us a burlesque in diction but not in sentiment
or character.[37]

In the second part of this portrait Fielding is still in the
introductory stages of his description. He exalts Sophia by
a series of flattering comparisons to the aristocratic subjects of famous portrait painters, and then by comparing
his heroine to his deceased wife, Charlotte. The first comparison associates Sophia with the Venus dei Medici, the
exemplary type of modest, maidenly beauty in the Augustan period.[38] The novelist also mentions the possibility of
comparing her to a number of contemporary British portraits: Kneller's famous full-length portraits at Hampton
Court and those of John Churchill's four daughters, exe-

cuted by the most prominent painters of the day. The implication in these references seems to be that though these models may not be capable of conveying an adequate idea of the heroine's perfections, the reader can construct his own preliminary and composite image of Sophia in much the same way as Reynolds directed his students to form a picture of ideal beauty.

Following these suggestions, Fielding says—in reference to the works of art just mentioned—"Now if thou hast seen all these, be not afraid of the rude answer which Lord Rochester once gave to a man, who had seen many things." C. J. Rawson tells us that the answer referred to is "If you have seen all this, then kiss mine A[rs]e," the last line of a poem titled "To all Curious Criticks and Admirers of Metre."[39] This rather bawdy reference adds a comic note to the portrait, changing its dignified, sublime tone to one that is iconoclastic and scurrilous. But because the reference is oblique and fleeting and does not involve Sophia directly but is addressed to the reader, it does not seem designed to diminish her status. Indeed the novelist, as we might expect, urges his reader to reject this cynicism from the pen of the notorious Rochester, whose unsentimental attitude toward women Fielding did not share.

The novelist then settles on two portraits which he says give strong likeness of Sophia: Kneller's full, sensual picture of Lady Ranelagh (a poised, striking woman) and Lely's full-bosomed duchess of Mazarine—but there is no evidence that his description was guided by either of these portraits. Certain details from each painting can be found in the sketch, but not the consistency that would be necessary to assume direct influence. More plausibly, his reference to these two portraits was designed to provide his reader with models who had been made ageless and idealized by art and whose dignified associations and exotic beauty would be transferred to the heroine.

These flattering comparisons, climaxed by an emotional identification of Sophia with the writer's deceased wife, are the prelude to the third section's detailed, systematic delineation of the heroine's physical beauty, in which she is presented by the idealized depiction that portrayed the traditional romance heroine. The anatomical catalogue is devoted chiefly to a minute examination of head and face, to which standard colors (rose and lily), shapes, and proportions are ascribed and in which the most conventional comparisons are employed (ivory, alabaster). The poetry of Suckling and Donne is used to describe Sophia's mouth and cheeks and to add idealizing, literary allusions to the visual description of these features.

The same process is operative in Fielding's allusion to the Venus dei Medici, for he tells us: "Her neck was long and finely turned; and here, if I was not afraid of offending her delicacy, I might justly say, the highest beauties of the famous *Venus de Medicis* were outdone." In the eighteenth century *la belle nature* was frequently conceived in sculpturesque terms;[40] Reynolds suggested that the artist turn to classical statuary to achieve the grandeur of generality and it became a common literary practice to represent idealized figures as classical marbles. So when Fielding has us see Sophia as the "moral Venus," he is doing much the same thing James Thomson did in his poetry much earlier in the century. Fielding is not, of course, verbally depicting the Venus and representing her as Sophia; that would not have been necessary. He merely refers us to the work of art and presumes that we will make the obvious connections.

To the Augustan age, the Venus dei Medici represented

"the standard of all female beauty and softness"—in the words of Joseph Spence—and so is a particularly apt work of art with which to exalt Sophia.[41] But there is a further point to the choice of Venus, for it was customary in the literary tradition in which Fielding is describing his heroine to mention only those parts of the body which are uncovered in contemporary dress. By this reference to the highest beauties of the Medici Venus, who in contrast to the Venus de Milo is entirely unclothed but modestly posed, Fielding was able to reveal and praise—in a subtle and decorous fashion—the most intimate charms of his heroine.

The bent of this description, as we have observed, is toward celebrating the greatest degree of grandeur without regard to the conventions of formal realism. In contrast to the various blemishes ascribed to Fanny, only one imperfection, a low forehead, is mentioned in this portrait of Sophia; and this generalized blemish, offered tentatively—indeed almost grudgingly—seems intended to tone down the superlative beauty of the heroine. At the same time, it is overwhelmed by the massive idealizing that informs the rest of the description.

Despite her extended depiction, Sophia, like Fielding's other heroes and heroines, is not presented as a person with a unique, distinctive appearance, and the reason she is not individualized can best be understood by comparing her with her father. It was Fielding's intention, in drawing Squire Western, to produce a humorous eccentric that would amuse the reader—what the eighteenth century would have considered "an original"—and he created a figure so full of idiosyncrasies that the squire is the closest to a unique individual in Fielding's prose fiction. In describing Sophia, however, his intent was radically different—to create a person whom the reader may respect and admire. Consequently, Sophia cannot be represented, in any significant respect, as an individual, as a divergence from the conventional ideal. As a major character in the novel, she must be truly universal and representative of a concept larger than her individuality; she must enshrine the perfect beauty of her sex and class.

Sophia's appearance is the most elaborate part of her portrait, and this description is followed by a generalized, almost vague sketch of her nature, which relies largely on exploiting the significance of what has already been said. Predictably, then, Sophia's exterior is emblematic of her mind; she is, as Martin Battestin argues, a type of virtue incarnate.[42] The point of Fielding's idealization, as her name would lead us to expect, is her objectification of the author's concept of wisdom. As an emblem of wisdom she plays—in addition to her realistic role—a semiallegorical part in which she is sought and ultimately won by the once imprudent Jones; and her marriage to Jones at the end of the novel signifies his symbolic acquisition of prudence,[43] resolving—if somewhat externally—the problem of his moral immaturity.

Sophia's portrait seems to end in the fourth section of the chapter, with a discussion of her education. In fact, however, the conclusion is an ironic sketch of the heroine's comic educator, Di Western, a worldly but discreet lady who has recently retired from court, whom Fielding intends as a contrast to Sophia. This versatile lady, moreover, is involved in more than one contrast, and she is introduced as the antithesis of her brother, Squire Western. "He was a man of no great observation. His sister was a lady of a different turn. She had lived about the Court, and had seen the world. Hence she had acquired all that knowledge which the said world usually communicates; and she was a perfect mistress of manners, customs, ceremonies, and fashions" (bk. 6, ch. 2). Squire Western's contrast to his sister is especially apt. Her devotion to the forms of court life, its manners, customs, and ceremonies, is startlingly remote from Western's semibarbarous existence, which is devoid of all but the crudest animal pleasures, and these in excess. The contrast is not just a reflection on the squire, however; both life styles are extreme. And the ironic tone in the reference to all the knowledge "which the said world usually communicates," coupled with the emphasis on jejune forms in a highly artificial life, points to the effete gentility and shallow sophistication of Mrs. Western.

Even Mrs. Western's intellectual interests are affected by her hollow formalism. The suggestion that she has a wide acquaintance with literature and history is intended ironically. Most of her reading matter—operas, romances, French memoirs, political pamphlets, and journals—is not just dilettantish but was considered by people like Hogarth and Fielding to be decadent and vicious forms of art. Nor are the results of her reading salutary. Her literary toil, instead of improving her, turns her into the worst of all creatures, a critic; and her study of pamphlets turns her into a female coffee-house politician.[44]

Not all of Mrs. Western's reading is ephemeral in value. However, her acquaintance with such substantive works as Rapin's *History of England* and her various other intellectual pretensions are undercut by the fact that she seems to consider her semiprurient interests in rumor and gossip on a plane with her intellectual interest. "She was moreover excellently well skilled in the doctrine of amour, and knew better than anybody who and who were together." The motive for this interest strips Fielding's Thalestris (as he calls her) of all pretension. She becomes a contrast to Sophia not just in the moral sphere but in her crudely caricatured physical appearance as well—which, predictably, is shown to be closely related to her ruling passion. Her knowledge of amour, Fielding tells us, was attained with facility because "her pursuit of it was never diverted by any affairs of her own; for either she had no inclinations, or they had never been solicited; which last is indeed very probable: for her masculine person, which was near six foot high, added to her manner and learning, possibly prevented the other sex from regarding her, notwithstanding her petticoats, in the light of a woman" (ibid.). Mrs. Western's first name, Diana, helps summarize these aspects of her character and fix them in the reader's mind. It associates her with the masculine figure of the huntress, so common in the visual arts, and establishes her as the unwilling patroness of virginity in *Tom Jones*.[45]

Recently, Mrs. Western has been considered an inconsistent figure, without recognizable coherence.[46] This criticism, however, does not adequately represent Fielding's intent and achievement in her creation. He presents her as a figure who has a basically good nature, but one that has been confounded and obscured by the false sophistication acquired in the city and at the court. But although her good nature has atrophied somewhat, it has not been destroyed. Her affectionate address to her brother (whom she does not "abandon") at the end of book 6, chapter 2, is ample proof of her warm nature. Sophia, convinced of her aunt's love for her brother, tells him that his sister has expressed "the greatest affection" for him "a thousand times." Mrs. Western's love for her niece is no less intense; she protects Sophia from her father's rage, releases her from captivity, and is kind to her according to her own lights. Sophia says of her: "I have great obligations to my aunt. She hath been a second mother to me." Mrs. Western, in short, is a woman who is good at heart, but she tries to hide a nature which she does not approve by an assumed, urbane decadence and an imitative cynicism.[47] She is not an inconsistent character; rather, she is a subtle, effective incarnation of the struggle of a cultured decadence that attempts to extinguish the best in her nature so as to give herself to an artificial ideal that she fails to realize is empty and worthless.

Ernest Baker sees Mrs. Western in another contrast in the novel. "In Miss Western, the prim feminism of the blue-stocking regime is a foil to the she-libertine, Lady Bellaston, typifying the profligacy of a certain aristocratic set."[48] This contrast is perhaps more coincidental than those we have thus far examined because the brief description of Lady Bellaston, which is confined entirely to the physical realities in which she deals, suggests little of this antithesis. Her portrait, which focuses on the reasons for Tom's difficulty in returning her passion, describes her as having

> now entered at least into the autumn of life; though she wore all the gayety of youth both in her dress and manner; nay, she contrived still to maintain the roses in her cheeks; but these, like flowers forced out of season by art, had none of the lively blooming freshness with which nature, at the proper time, bedecks her own productions. She had, besides, a certain imperfection, which renders some flowers, tho' very beautiful to the eye, very improper to be placed in a wilderness of sweets, and what above all others is more disagreeable to the breath of love. (Bk. 13, ch. 9)

If a contrast is intended, even implicitly, by this description, it is not between Lady Bellaston and Mrs. Western but between her ladyship and Sophia, who is mentioned just prior to the sketch as Tom's true love. Bellaston's description is composed of a selection of the qualities that make up Sophia's appearance (gaiety, youth, rosy cheeks). The effect of these details is reversed, however, and they are associated with images of corruption and death. The ultimate result is a description of Bellaston as a figure whose decaying façade masks the physical signs of bodily and spiritual rot. This portrait is an accurate index to her realization in the plot. She is a Lady Booby grown older, more practiced and unscrupulous in her affairs, and more cynical, manipulative, and vicious in her outlook.

Between Bridget Allworthy and Mrs. Western there is a more calculated contrast and one which is much more basic to Fielding's thematic interests in *Tom Jones* than the one between Lady Bellaston and Mrs. Western. Both women live with their brothers in the country and come from the same social and economic class. Like Mrs. Western, Bridget is "somewhat past the age of thirty" and is rather ugly. But a key difference between the two is emphasized in the loose Theophrastan sketch that depicts the latter by the rather novel method of recording her own words and her neighbors' sentiments about her.

> She was of that species of woman, whom you rather commend for good qualities than beauty, and who are generally called by their own sex, very good sort of women—as good a sort of woman, madam, as you would wish to know. Indeed, she was so far from regretting want of beauty, that she never mention'd that perfec-

tion (if it can be called one) without contempt; and would often thank God she was not as handsome as Miss such a one, whom perhaps beauty had led into errors, which she might otherwise have avoided. (Bk. 1, ch. 2)

It is in the different compensatory reactions of the two women to their lack of beauty that the difference between them appears and by virtue of which each becomes representative of an antithesis that permeates the novel. Mrs. Western, who has what Fielding frequently calls "a town education," compensates for her appearance by a vicarious interest in others' affairs, which affirms the morality of such amours. Bridget, who has spent her entire life in the country, has affairs of her own, but hides her interest in sexual matters behind a moralistic pose.

This attitude is the center of Bridget's ethos. She is presented as a humor character of a simple kind: the moralistic, hypocritical old maid. Careful not to suggest that she is an individual, Fielding introduces her as "that species of woman" and describes the type rather than Bridget herself. This broad "type characterization" occurs much less frequently in *Tom Jones* than in *Joseph Andrews*, and Fielding used it only for special effects. With Bridget, the novelist seems to insist on rigid conformity to type so that the reader can respond to the irony in her strangely favorable reaction to the arrival of a bastard in her house. Fielding fulfills our expectation of Bridget's reaction when he details the behavior of Deborah Wilkins, who is a stand-in for Bridget. An equally moralistic old maid, she can be relied on to ape what she predicts will be her mistress's response. The reader is intended to share the maid's bewilderment at

Bridget Allworthy's uncharacteristic behavior and to seek—beyond the speculations the narrator speciously advances—the reasons for this violation of decorum.

The action of the novel adds new dimensions to Bridget's character and complexity to her initially stereotyped portrait. As Sheridan Baker points out:

> The Old Maid—unattractive, sour, hostile to beauty as an enemy of virginity—soon reveals herself as a Learned Lady too: her theological discussions lead first to marriage with Captain Blifil then to intellectual contempt for him, both attitudes demanded by the plot. Soon she shows all the symptoms of the Amorous Matron—of whom Congreve's Lady Wishfort is perhaps the archetype—a lady, in Fielding's books, usually married or widowed (as Bridget in natural fact is), moved to sexual indiscretion with younger men by the weight of about 40 winters.[49]

As she works through these roles in the action of the novel (occasionally even transcending them), she is shrewdly observed "with enough vigor among seeming inconsistencies to suggest that if we knew her thoroughly she would seem thoroughly authentic, a unique individual yet thoroughly representative of the several typical roles life has put upon her."[50]

Fielding's idea for this complex character, R. E. Moore suggests, came directly from Hogarth's *Morning*.[51] Moore bases this assertion on a passage that occurs long after the novelist has described Bridget's character: "This lady, no more than her lover, was remarkable for beauty. I would attempt to draw her picture; but that is done already by a more able master, Mr Hogarth himself, to whom she sat many years ago, and hath been lately exhibited by that gentleman in his print of a Winter's Morning, of which he was no improper emblem, and may be seen walking (for walk she doth in the print) to Covent-Garden church, with a starved foot-boy behind carrying her prayer-book" (bk. 1, ch. 11). Fielding's choice of the woman in *Morning* as an analogue to Bridget is apt. Hogarth's figure, somewhat beyond her prime, is disaffected, ugly, and humorless. Her ostentatious piousness and her hypocrisy are contrasted with the healthy sexuality of the two young girls she regards so disapprovingly. But while Hogarth's figure echoes some of Bridget's important traits, this fact cannot be taken as an indication that Fielding used the artist's work as the source of his characterization of Bridget Allworthy. There is no evidence that Fielding had Hogarth's figure in mind in his initial description of Bridget. Her character, as the last paragraph makes clear, develops in response to the novel's plot, and with a complexity that Hogarth's figure cannot represent.

How, then, does this reference to Hogarth function at this point in the novel? Fielding has set up this chapter so as to introduce, at this point, a visual representation of Bridget. He has just given us a full picture of Captain Blifil's odd appearance, and to indicate the perfect matching of this unromantic pair Fielding sets the mistress beside the lover ("The lady, no more than her lover, was remarkable for beauty")—in a type of verbal *American Gothic*. Instead of describing Bridget as he has the captain, he refers us to Hogarth's powerful portrait.

His treatment of the captain's appearance is very different: Bridget's mate is presented by a verbal portrait that is both effective and direct.

This gentleman was about 35 years of age. He was of a middle size, and what is called well built. He had a scar on his forehead, which did not so much injure his beauty, as it denoted his valour (for he was a half-pay officer.) He had good teeth, and something affable, when he pleased in his smile; though naturally his countenance, as well as his air and voice, had much of roughness in it, yet he could at any time deposit this, and appear all gentleness and good humour. He was not ungenteel, not entirely void of wit, and in his youth had abounded in spriteliness, which, though he had lately put on a more serious character, he could, when he pleased, resume. (Bk. 1, ch. 10)

The captain owed nothing to any of these fop-makers in his dress, nor was his person much more beholden to nature. Both his dress and his person were such as, had they appeared in an assembly, or a drawing-room, would have been the contempt and ridicule of all the fine ladies there. The former of these was indeed neat, but plain, coarse, ill-fancied, and out of fashion. As for the latter, we have expressly described it above. So far was the skin on his cheeks from being cherry-coloured, that you could not discern what the natural colour of his cheeks was, they being totally overgrown by a black beard, which ascended to his eyes. His shape and limbs were indeed exactly proportioned, but so large, that they denoted the strength rather of a ploughman than any other. His shoulders were broad, beyond all size, and the calves of his legs larger than those of a common chairman. In short, his whole person wanted all that elegance and beauty, which is the very reverse of clumsy strength, and which so agreeably sets off most of our fine gentlemen; being partly owing to the high blood of their ancestors. (Bk. 1, ch. 11)

Captain Blifil is treated at greater length than his part in the novel seems to merit because Fielding appears to have become involved in his conception of Blifil and in realizing the figure as fully as he was able. This portrait, in contrast to similar ones in *Joseph Andrews*, is closer to caricature than to emblematic description. In the captain's portrait caricature the details of his appearance, described in specific terms, are ugly, bizarre, and distorted, though they are all natural. Blifil has none of the physical beauty of Fielding's real gentlemen. Indeed, the captain's appearance is something of a contrast to, if not the reverse of, Tom Jones's and Joseph Andrews's, telling us that Blifil is not an aristocrat but is unrefined and common.

Fielding even goes beyond this, suggesting that Blifil is not just common and unattractive but alarmingly singular and grotesque. First, he indicates that the captain's body is somewhat deformed: it is not much "beholden to nature." Even in the praise bestowed on him, a slur is implied in telling us the captain's teeth are good, for Fielding seems to judge him as he would a horse.

Fielding, though describing the captain's appearance in detail, gives us little analysis of his character. Instead, he gives us Blifil's epitaph (written by "a great genius" and "one who perfectly well knew the captain").

Here lies,
In Expectation of a joyful Rising,
The Body of
Captain JOHN BLIFIL.
London
Had the Honour of his Birth,
Oxford
of his Education.
His Parts
were an Honour to his Profession
and to his Country:

His Life to his Religion
and human Nature.
He was a dutiful Son,
a tender Husband,
an affectionate Father,
a most kind Brother,
a sincere Friend,
a devout Christian,
and a good Man.
His inconsolable Widow
hath erected this Stone,
The Monument of
His Virtues
and of Her Affection.

In reading this epitaph the reader is supposed to see Blifil's tombstone, no doubt, as a type of *memento mori*. The form of the writing—its layout and typography— suggest the long stone on which the sentiments are engraved. It is, as well, a short biographical character sketch, written in accord with the rhetorical formula for praise and blame, a formula frequently used for panegyrical funeral orations, and it has this function here. However, everything in it is intended ironically, and instead of being a piece of elegaic praise is a final, dooming condemnation.

III

Though its presence and importance in *Tom Jones* are evident in what we have said, literary portraiture in Fielding's novels is richest and most varied in *Joseph Andrews*. At the same time, however, the nature of Fielding's characterization has changed. His figures are still tied to his ethical system, but the ideals of that system, as they are embodied in the characters, seem no longer as absolute and cerebral.

In general, Fielding moves away from ethical types in *Tom Jones*, creating, instead, a large number and wide range of social and psychological studies. This change is evident in such people as Di Western, Lady Bellaston, Squire Western, and Mrs. Waters. Very few people in this novel have predominantly ethical functions. And unlike the situation in *Jonathan Wild* and *Joseph Andrews*, these central ethical figures are not major characters, like Adams and Wild, but minor ones, like Thwackum, Square, and Allworthy. Tom, for example, is a paragon only in a limited and somewhat sentimental sense. Significant names are the best index to this development: in *Tom Jones* the use of such names—greatly reduced from *Joseph Andrews*—is restricted to a small number of minor personages.

This change in the nature and techniques of Fielding's characterization is accompanied by a decline in the use of his major forms of direct literary portraiture. Only limited use is made of elaborate descriptive conventions in his 1749 novel. There is no emblematic portraiture, and only one really full-length idealized delineation. Except for Captain Blifil's epitaph, it does not employ the biographical character sketch in its full form, and it makes only limited use of the direct character sketch. Fewer figures are described by this device in *Tom Jones* than in *Joseph Andrews* and *Jonathan Wild*. The form and uses of the direct sketch also change: psychological characterization is not presented in unified, full, set-piece delineations of personality but in numerous two- and three-sentence passages that are dispersed throughout the novel.

As a result of the diminished place of direct literary portraiture, some of the earlier character depiction is replaced by other aspects of the novels, specifically by plot and dialogue. Delineation by plot and dialogue tends to make characterization an ongoing process, not something begun and concluded within the boundaries of a single sketch. In contrast to direct portraits, which stress what is uniform and typical about human nature, extended dramatic characterization emphasizes what is unique and particular.

One of the reasons for critics' difficulties and controversies over Fielding's portraiture in *Tom Jones* is that the characterization is in transition between the two antithetic modes of depiction mentioned above. For while the function of plot and dialogue has increased, literary portraiture still plays an important role. As a result, both modes of presentation are reflected in his characterization, and Fielding's personages embody what is both permanent and transient and particular and general in human nature. On the one hand, then, the reader must reject that analysis of Fielding's figures which sees all of them as "as real and lifelike as any in literature" when this means that all the characters in *Tom Jones* are unique individuals. On the other hand, the reader must also reject analyses which would flatten and reduce Fielding's personages to character types. Even the most sensitive and useful attempts to classify the figures in *Tom Jones* must be regarded with skepticism. Few will deny the aptness of the "walking concept" to Thwackum, but can it be applied equally well to Square in light of the change he undergoes after being discovered with Molly and his instructive but humanly plausible reformation? Only those analyses and judgments which embrace both aspects of Fielding's characterization can illuminate his achievement.

It is obvious, therefore, that depiction by direct portraiture in Fielding's novels tends to preclude further investigation and development of character. In *Jonathan Wild* and *Joseph Andrews*, for example, once a figure's nature has been described it generally remains fixed within the moral and psychological boundaries in which it was first presented. If, however, such boundaries are not set or are established only loosely, as is frequently the case in *Tom Jones*, the personages so described tend to change and develop. In a word, there is generally an inverse relationship between the fullness of a character's literary portrait and the uniqueness of his personality. This principle has interesting implications for Fielding's final novel, *Amelia*, in which direct portraiture is virtually nonexistent.

CHAPTER FIVE

Amelia

$\mathcal{B}$ETWEEN THE PUBLICATION of *Tom Jones* and *Amelia* the nature of Fielding's moral intentions deepened profoundly and inevitably, so did the means he chose to realize his intensified ethical purposes. Impressed by the social problems he daily encountered as a justice of the peace (he was one of the best and most dedicated of the period), he seems to have felt an immediate necessity "to promote the cause of virtue, and to expose some of the most glaring evils, as well public as private, which at present infest the country" (*Amelia*, preface). It is in this reformist spirit that Fielding conceived *Amelia*.

Published at the same time as he was writing pamphlets on such topics as the increasing crime rate and the providential detection of murderers, *Amelia* was intended to appeal to a broadly psychological and social awareness, rather than an intellectual consciousness, and where he had previously attempted to educate the mind, he now tries to affect the heart. He abandoned his cerebral, comic mode and all its adjuncts: its impartiality, restraint, mockery, aesthetic distance, skepticism, and irony. In place of double-edged comedy, he adopted a practical rhetoric that is serious in tone, that is consciously one-sided, committed, sentimental, and middle class.

This change in modes can be seen in a preliminary way in the differences between Allworthy and Harrison, the paragons of his last two novels. Allworthy, living in Paradise Hall on his country estate, is removed from the world. He surveys it from above and enters it only as the agent of an evenhanded, reasonable justice. He is apolitical and professionally nonpartisan, and even his religion is that of an educated, philosophic man. Harrison, who does not have the same balanced temperament as Allworthy, inclines violently to religious and political reform and is willingly embroiled in the struggle. He is not impartial but is consciously one-sided and resolutely partisan.[1] It is evident from this capsule analysis of these two representative figures that Fielding's characters in *Amelia* are more fiery, vehement, and immediate embodiments of his beliefs and concerns than the figures in his earlier works. Abandoning his magisterial role as narrator-director and reducing the aesthetic distance between himself and his characters, he seems to live and act directly in them in *Amelia*.

I

The characters the reader encounters in the opening chapters of *Amelia* provide the first indications of the effects of Fielding's intensified moral impulses and somber tone. The work opens in much the same way as the writer's previous stories, as the familiar, commanding narrator steps forward to propose his subject matter and discuss its nuances in a preliminary chapter. The tale itself, again rather typically, begins in the second chapter, as the narrator relates his story "after our usual manner," with many of his characteristic interruptions, digressions, and addresses to the reader.

The characters that are introduced in book 1 of *Amelia* and the descriptive techniques that are used to present them are rather easily recognizable products of the novelist's characteristic mode. Two such satiric personages, surrounded by a number of satellite characters, dominate the first book, and we shall begin our discussion of literary portraiture in *Amelia* by looking at these figures.

The first to appear is Justice Jonathan Thrasher, the magistrate before whom Booth is brought for "assaulting" a watchman.

> Mr. Thrasher, however, the justice before whom the prisoners above mentioned were now brought, had some few imperfections in his magistratical capacity. I own I have been sometimes inclined to think that this office of a justice of peace requires some knowledge of the law, for this simple reason: because, in every case which comes before him, he is to judge and act according to law. Again, as these laws are contained in a great variety of books, the statutes which relate to the office of a justice of peace making themselves at least two large volumes in folio; and that part of his jurisdiction which is founded on the common law being dispersed in above a hundred volumes, I cannot conceive how this knowledge should be acquired without reading; and yet certain is it, Mr. Thrasher never read one syllable of the matter.
>
> This perhaps was a defect; but this was not all: for where mere ignorance is to decide a point between two litigants, it will always be an even chance whether it decides right or wrong; but sorry am I to say, right was often in a much worse situation than this, and wrong hath often had five hundred to one on his side before

that magistrate, who, if he was ignorant of the laws of England, was yet well versed in the laws of nature. He perfectly well understood that fundamental principle so strongly laid down in the institutes of the learned Rochefoucault, by which the duty of self-love is so strongly enforced, and every man is taught to consider himself as the centre of gravity, and to attract all things thither. To speak the truth plainly, the justice was never indifferent in a cause but when he could get nothing on either side. (Bk. 1, ch. 2)

The narrator is quite prominent throughout this sketch; instead of the usual playful figure, however, he is openly and consistently condemnatory of his subject and employs a tone that borders on the sentimental and moralistic ("but sorry am I to say"). Despite this tone, there is much that is typical of a Fielding character in the form and content of this sketch. The novelist relies on the crude, significant name to indicate, prior to formal characterization, the figure's basic moral nature; then he outlines the relevant elements of Thrasher's nature in a psychological character sketch. He describes Thrasher as venal and illiterate, and defines these qualities not as character deficiencies but as corrupting influences on the judge's administration of public office. Fielding has taken the traditional type-character, which in its earliest form was a vehicle for his abstract ethical theses, and transformed it into a device for expressing his intensified social awareness.

Fielding's novels are full of magistrates, and the contrast between Thrasher and an earlier justice, the figure in *Joseph Andrews* before whom Adams and Fanny are brought, is instructive. The principal characteristic of the magistrate in *Joseph Andrews* is his illiteracy. Treated hu-

morously, the illiteracy is made the subject of a witty re-
partee that reflects on Adams's learning and the magistrate's ignorance. Thrasher too is illiterate, but in *Amelia*
this fact is not treated humorously; it is expressed only in
terms of its social implication—in terms of the "imperfections in his magistratical capacity." Thrasher's venality is
seen exclusively as a perversion of social justice. Fielding's
light irony and playful burlesque, long associated with
the depiction of such secondary figures, are gone. Presented in this novel in a heavy-handed and overtly didactic manner, in which even the humorless irony becomes
moralistic, these figures indicate some of the changes in
Fielding's tone.

All the most vivid characters in book 1 appear in the
prison scene. Although the masquerade at Ranelagh has
been considered the equivalent of the lower world in the
Aeneid,[2] Fielding's prison may be much more convincingly identified with Aeneas's underworld. The gloomy
place is full of grotesque creatures that come to Booth
and greet him with various petitions, and the prison itself
is a type of earthly hell. Fielding, aware of the epic implications of his words, describes it as "these (not improp-
erly called infernal) regions."

The hellish population of this region most concerns us
here. The first person who greets Booth is undoubtedly
the most powerful grotesque in the entire novel.

The first person who accosted him was called Blear-
eyed Moll, a woman of no very comely appearance.
Her eye (for she had but one), whence she derived her
nickname, was such as that nickname bespoke; besides
which, it had two remarkable qualities; for first, as if
Nature had been careful to provide for her own defect,

it constantly looked towards her blind side; and secondly, the ball consisted almost entirely of white, or
rather yellow, with a little grey spot in the corner, so
small that it was scarce discernible. Nose she had none,
for Venus, envious perhaps at her former charms, had
carried off the gristly part, and some earthly damsel,
perhaps from the same envy, had levelled the bone with
the rest of her face: indeed it was far beneath the bones
of her cheeks, which rose proportionally higher than is
usual. About half a dozen ebony teeth fortified that
large and long canal which nature had cut from ear to
ear, at the bottom of which was a chin preposterously
short, nature having turned up the bottom instead of
suffering it to grow to its due length.

Her body was well adapted to her face; she mea-
sured full as much round the middle as from head to
foot; for, besides the extreme breadth of her back, her
vast breasts had long since forsaken their native home,
and had settled themselves a little below the girdle. . . .
[N]othing more ragged or more dirty was ever emptied out of the round-house at St. Giles's. (Bk. 1, ch. 3)

Whether this sketch was influenced by Hogarth's work
is difficult to say. In plate 7 of *A Rake's Progress* (1735)
there is an interesting visual analogue to Moll,[3] in which
the imprisoned Rakewell is confronted by his enraged
wife, who is not unlike Moll in appearance. Mrs. Rakewell has one eye that squints in the direction of her blind
side. Her nose is not damaged, like Moll's, but she has
the same sparse collection of teeth, the same wide mouth,
and the same short chin. In stature, too, both women are
similar: each is short and rotund. These resemblances,
however, are not so remarkable as to unequivocally posit
a direct influence. The most that can be said is that the
similarities between Moll and Mrs. Rakewell suggest that

Hogarth's *Rake's Progress* may have inspired the novelist's visualization of Moll. It also seems likely that Fielding borrowed the details of stature and facial peculiarities from his friend's work. But more important than such specific parallels are the "echoes" from Hogarth's engravings which critics like Robert E. Moore have noted, and especially those that pertain to Fielding's grotesque characters and suggest that the empirical impulse in the writer's descriptive technique is in part due to the visual artist's delineations.

Our discussions of the relationship between Fielding and Hogarth have no doubt given the impression that the work of these artists is fundamentally alike, and in general this impression is correct. Both men worked with middle-class art forms, the novel and the engraving, and both were moralists. A blend of comic and satiric elements, their work is distinguished by its commitment to the promotion of virtue and the exposure of political, social, personal, and artistic corruption. Both use their characters as vehicles for these purposes, and as a result they created broadly similar figures. Hogarth's characters, like so many of Fielding's, are social and psychological stereotypes with obvious moral dimensions. This kinship is accurately revealed by the former's use of the same type of significant names as the novelist employed: Tom Rakewell, Moll Hackabout, Lawyer Silvertongue, and the like.

Within this broad didactic tradition, however, there are important differences. While Fielding was concerned with the nature and operation of personality and how these are affected by different circumstances, Hogarth was interested in questions of moral choice and consequence and the individual and social forces that act on human nature in such situations. The latter is fatalistic, documentary, and literal and his work is concerned with matters that have broad social dimensions. Sharply focused in both subject matter and purpose, Hogarth is, above all, a rigorous and programmatic moralist, and with the exception of some early pieces his work is a direct expression and promotion (sometimes to the point of propaganda) of middle-class attitudes, values, and aspirations. Fielding's art is not so class bound as Hogarth's; its values are more cosmopolitan and it is consistently more secular, less blunt, and more indirect in working out its moral purposes. Avowedly tolerant, the novelist reflects a more ambiguous moral vision. While Fielding is at his most compelling in depicting such models as Adams and Jones, Hogarth, whose imagination was profoundly negative, paints vice more vividly and convincingly than virtue. Interestingly enough, the novelist seems to have been aware of this propensity in his friend for he identifies only his rogues and villains (like Moll) with characters in Hogarth's works.

Whatever its relationship to Hogarth, Moll's description stands by itself as a vivid, detailed picture. Revealing Fielding's new interest in the possibilities of literal description, her portrait is not so much a literary caricature as a grotesque, almost photographic representation of a degraded woman. Still, with its concentrated description of Moll's face, it also seems designed in contrast to the idealized model Fielding used to depict ladies like Sophia. Each feature of the wretch's face is reported in such a manner as to travesty a detail from the easily remembered and idealized mode of depiction. For example, the full, perfectly even, ivory-color teeth of Fielding's standard heroine become half a dozen ebony weapons fortifying a canal. Some of the details in Moll's description, however, have a very literal significance of their own and suggest specific aspects of her personality. Her missing nose, whose loss is comically narrated, is a reference to her promiscuity and her contentious disposition. Her one eye ("a little grey spot in the corner, so small that it was scarce discernible") and its erratic cant also suggests her distorted moral vision.

Up to the very last sentence of this portrait Fielding makes no explicit or editorial comment on his subject; but he concludes Moll's depiction with the same type of didactic intrusion we have seen in Thrasher's portrait. His attitude toward criminals and social misfits was then so intense and committed that he breaks the neutral tone of the sketch and ends by attacking his character in a way he would never have attacked Slipslop or Tow-wouse. "Nothing more ragged or more dirty," he says, "was ever emptied out of the round-house at St. Giles's."

Book 1 of *Amelia* can best be described as a set piece on prisons and their inhabitants—a verbal showcase of social evil. Its concentration of grotesque figures, many of them depicted most vividly, is designed to affect the reader viscerally. With the exception of the figures just discussed, these personages are not presented in character sketches, nor do they have genuine interest as characters. They are intended exclusively as *exempla* for a series of points that Fielding wishes to make about human nature and English law. The following passage, for example, in which the novelist describes the plight of a young girl, is representative.

> They now beheld a little creature sitting by herself in a corner, and crying bitterly. This girl, Mr. Robinson

said, was committed because her father-in-law, who was in the grenadier guards, had sworn that he was afraid of his life, or of some bodily harm which she would do him, and she could get no sureties for keeping the peace; for which reason justice Thrasher had committed her to prison. (Bk. 1, ch. 4)

There is no interest in the girl's character; the whole point of the description is to indicate that the law is open to manipulation by the rich against the poor, who are usually without protection or recourse.

The following description serves much the same purpose; only the theme is different.

A very pretty girl then advanced toward them, whose beauty Mr. Booth could not help admiring the moment he saw her, declaring, at the same time, he thought she had great innocence in her countenance. Robinson said she was committed thither as an idle and disorderly person, and a common street-walker. As she passed by Mr. Booth she damned his eyes and discharged a volley of words, every one of which was too indecent to be repeated. (Ibid.)

Again, the interest is not in character; it is in presenting, at the outset of the novel, the thesis that people can be physically beautiful but morally corrupt, which is an important point in *Amelia* and a characteristic thesis of this novel. The reverse, that the ugly may be virtuous, Fielding (and few other writers) never fully suggests. For the most part, however, these vignettes are of little relevance to this study and we will pass them over to describe Fielding's characterization in the rest of *Amelia*.

II

As we have observed about *Amelia*, Fielding abandoned much of the characteristic aesthetic distance between himself and his characters to act and speak more directly in and through them than in his previous novels. This results in a new kind of immediacy and closeness between the novel's characters and the writer's ideological concerns, and the cost of this immediacy or fidelity is the rejection of almost all formal conventions of character drawing. *Amelia* is substantially without direct literary portraiture of the kind we found in Fielding's first three works of prose fiction.

In a real sense, then, the principal concerns of this study are not strictly applicable to Fielding's last novel; yet any change in his portraiture, even if it is not within the sharply defined boundaries of this investigation, should be examined both for the light it may throw on his general characterization and on the nature and direction of its development. Following Fielding's lead, the rest of this chapter will widen the focus of the early part of this study and examine larger questions of characterization in *Amelia*, attempting to show how and why specific features of the writer's earlier portraiture disappear and the consequent effects.

One of the first things we notice when we move into the body of this novel is that the narrator does not develop into the familiar, genial, omnipresent storyteller of *Tom Jones*. Instead of acting as the all-knowing director-narrator who variously creates, classifies, and describes his characters, he operates on such a reduced scale that he is almost unnoticed.[4] Humble and retiring, he is a plain, blunt man who tells a simple story.[5] It is not by accident that, speaking of *Amelia* in *The Covent-Garden Journal,* Fielding characterized the storyteller in this novel as an "old Gentleman" and "a grave Man."[6]

This narrator also operates differently within the world he is telling us about. Instead of an omniscient creator who, as Aurelien Digeon points out, claims to control reality and select from it,[7] and who is responsible for the characters of the earlier novels, the narrator in *Amelia* is familiar with the world the story occurs in, but he did not create that world and he cannot manipulate it. Like the reader, he is an observer who merely records its history.[8] The reduced nature and function of this narrator also suggests something of the related changes in *Amelia's* methods of characterization. In *Joseph Andrews* and *Tom Jones* the narrator is the agent by which reality is presented deductively; he knows everything that is important to the story *a priori.* His methods are abstract and summary and his omniscient knowledge of characters, organized into conclusions, generalizations, and intellectual patterns, is set forth in condensed, highly organized, and even consciously literary forms.

In *Amelia,* reality is approached inductively through an empirically minded, retiring figure who observes and records things as they occur. The first effect of this approach on the novel's characterization is that figures are presented in the cumulative, gradual manner in which people frequently get to know one another. With a few insignificant exceptions, set biographies, Theophrastan analyses, and "characters" of people disappear. Figures are introduced by degrees and we get to know them through their speech and action and the opinions others hold of them—evaluating each character at each appearance and often making new discoveries and assessments about them.[9] Equally important, these assessments are not made explicit through an intermediary; they are formulated by the reader. Decorum is no longer a controlling principle of characterization; fidelity to human experience, as a changing phenomenon, is the touchstone of reality in *Amelia*. Characters may change, as Booth's developing attitude toward religion indicates. They may also reveal unexpected aspects of themselves under different circumstances, and as a result there are surprises in *Amelia*, but not the same kind we see in *Tom Jones* and *Joseph Andrews*. More subtle in nature, the surprises in Fielding's last novel tend to be concerned with psychological changes, or with the reader's knowledge of the moral nature of the personages, and not with sudden transformations in their social and economic circumstances though these also occur.

The author's treatment of external appearance also changes in *Amelia*. Little attention is paid to details of appearance, and even less importance attached to them. Significantly, beauty and ugliness are no longer used as incontrovertible manifestations of a figure's moral nature. Nor do virtue or vice find expression in the elaborate catalogues of beauty and deformity that characterized the earlier novels; they are generally manifested in brief descriptions of facial expression. An obvious corollary pertaining to a related aspect of literary portraiture follows from this diminished interest in physical appearance. Fielding usually established emblematic characters by shaping natural, visual details into a recognizable icon, but in the absence of details of natural appearance the medium for iconic or emblematic representation disappears, and with it these dimensions of his characterization. In general, Fielding's art has become increasingly literal and experimental, so that many of his former modes of depiction, with their pronounced literary associations and functions, are no longer of any use to him.

The shift from the narrator's shaping vision to a less embellished, more literal mode also correlates with changes in the patterns in which characters relate to one another. In the previous novels they generally appeared in sharp, formal opposition and they embodied symmetrical points of view in distinct antithesis. In *Amelia*, these highly intellectual, purposefully artificial patterns have faded out and only their traces remain. Where character contrasts exist (Amelia–Mrs. Bennet, Amelia–Booth, Booth–Atkinson), they are no longer tied to one-dimensional relationships that are based on simple ethical or psychological factors; instead, they are so obliquely managed as to appear almost artless.

Inasmuch as the new emphasis on change and fluctuation destroys the possibilities for simple formal contrasts between characters, the semiallegorical relationships that are founded on contrasting moral viewpoints inevitably disappear. Characters in *Amelia* exist in a social, not an intellectual, milieu. They are seen as part of a human family, or as a small, intimate society, and the intricate personal relationships generated in these groups are as much a part of this novel as the intellectual or moral relationships were part of the earlier works.

Perhaps the best way to understand the changes in Fielding's methods of characterization is to look at how they are realized in a number of examples. Although Mrs. Bennet has been described as the character in whom the possibilities of Fielding's new techniques are most successfully and most thoroughly realized, she is not an unrepresentative figure in *Amelia*, and many of the techniques by which she is presented are used for all the major figures in the book.

This lady enters the story unobtrusively in book 4. Only the most casual mention (and a depreciating one at that) is made of her appearance: "Sickness had given her an older look, and had a good deal diminished her beauty; of which, young as she was, she plainly appeared to have only the remains in her present possession" (bk. 4, ch. 9). There is no set-piece description or judgment of her nature; she is introduced to make a fourth at whist (with Mrs. Ellison and the Booths), and she appears as a grave young woman with a mysterious, unhappy past. She next appears, again unobtrusively, on two social occasions at Mrs. Ellison's apartment, where she says almost nothing. After these visits, Booth and Amelia speak of the favorable impression this strange woman has made on them. Then, for a considerable period, Mrs. Bennet disappears from the novel. When she reappears, Mrs. Ellison gives a more detailed account of the young woman's recent misfortunes. Then the lady herself steps in to save Amelia from the noble lord, tells her long story, dominates Booth's and Amelia's lives for a time, and becomes a major character in the novel.

All the important characters in the book are presented in the same fashion as Mrs. Bennet. There is no character sketch and no physical description of Booth, the novel's principal male protagonist. Unlike Fielding's earlier, straightforward narratives, *Amelia* begins *in medias res* and Booth appears without the familiar introductory capsule biography that takes the reader from his parentage through his birth and early education. Indeed, the hero appears in the second chapter of book 1, already married to the heroine, and it is only after his experience with the class nature of British justice that we begin to know him. And, significantly, what we learn of his past comes not from the narrator but from Booth's own lips, in his conversations with other figures.

Amelia is treated in the same way. On a number of occasions she is described by her facial reactions to situations which bring pain or joy; but in contrast to Fielding's elaborations on the beauty of the heroines of his earlier works, such as Fanny and Sophia, the "great beauty" of the heroine of *Amelia* is never delineated. Indeed, Fielding permits Amelia's appearance to be marred by a serious injury to her nose (permanently in the first edition, temporarily in later editions). Moreover, there is a daring contrast between the blear-eyed Moll, whose damaged nose is a direct result and external representation of her sexual amorality, and Amelia, whose nose is damaged by an accident resulting in a scar that is quite incidental to her character.

It is equally significant that the reader's limited knowledge of the heroine's appearance suggests that she may be lacking in ideal beauty. In a critique of Amelia's appearance (which does not stand apart from the narrative as a set piece but is contained in a dialogue), Mrs. James compares the heroine's features to the contemporary standards of ideal beauty and finds her lacking. This critique, aimed at Mrs. James's husband, is undeniably partisan, and may tell as much about her mercurial disposition as it does about Amelia's appearance, but, in the absence of other description, this depiction, together with the scar, inevitably raises questions about Amelia's absolute beauty and the relevance—in Fielding's view—of such standards of beauty. This point seems especially valid when we remember the "very pretty girl" who was sent to prison as "an idle and disorderly person, and a common street-walker."

In *Amelia*, as we have seen, the narrator does not segregate the reader and the characters. Instead of reading about taxonomic aspects that are perceived by the categorizing mind of an intermediary, the reader is in direct contact with each figure through his words and deeds. He listens to the main characters as they tell their own life stories and explain their motives in their own words. As a result, the distance between the characters and the reader decreases and the personages in *Amelia* appear more as individuals than as types. There are very few idiosyncratic figures and humor characters in the work. Indeed, as F. Holmes Dudden remarks, "with the exception of Colonel Bath, there are no eccentrics. The extravagant, the fanciful, the unusual in characterization is avoided."[10] Normal, unexceptional, domestic middle-class people, most figures in *Amelia*, at least on the surface, are presented independently of overt stereotypes.

Emphasis on types or on individuals is usually evident in a novelist's choice of characters' names, and while Fielding's characters generally have significant names, type names are employed in *Amelia* only for figures who appear momentarily, to make a point and then vanish, such as Thrasher, Bondum, and Constable Gotbed. All the main characters, and most of the minor ones (like Robinson, Hebbers, Murphy, Carey, and so on), have common names that are devoid of any intimation of special significance. "Amelia," for example, was one of the commonest "polite" names of the day, and so ordinary are the names of the other principal characters that it has been suggested that Fielding took most of them at random from a printed list of contemporaries. The surnames Booth, Matthews,

Harrison, Atkinson, Trent, and Bennet are in the list of subscribers to a 1724 folio edition of Burnet's *History of His Own Time*, of which Fielding owned a copy.[11]

Finally, we must look at how character development or change is affected by the absence of devices and techniques that are often associated with type characterization. And again, the remarkable Mrs. Bennet is *Amelia's* most successful example of Fielding's interest in new aspects of character.[12] As we have observed, she first appears as a docile, passive person, prematurely aged by an unfortunate experience, and thus she evokes our pity. However, our response is somewhat modified by her next appearance, as a gay, good-humored female pedant who delivers a speech against second marriages with grace and learning—to which Booth and his wife assent "rather out of complaisance than from their real judgment." Also, her long autobiography further complicates her assessment. Although she seems, for most of her story, the victim of an unkind fortune and a cruel world that is determined to undo her, several questions arise about her integrity. When she tells us about her attempts to save her father from the arms of her future stepmother, we are aware that Mrs. Bennet is telling the story and that such tales of family disagreement are rarely as straightforward as she would have Amelia believe.

At least one critic has also observed that her tale about her courtship and marriage to a clergyman is open to an unflattering interpretation. Below is Mrs. Bennet's account of her surrender to the man who was to become her first husband: "He did this [press his suit] in so forcible though gentle a manner, with such a profusion of fervency and tenderness at once, that his love, like a torrent, bore everything before it; and I am almost ashamed to own to you how very soon he prevailed upon me to—to—in short, to be an honest woman, and to confess to him the plain truth" (bk. 7, ch. 5). J. S. Coolidge suggests an interesting interpretation of this account.

> Her sentence seems pretty obviously to be leading up to an event upon which, in Fielding's customary phrase, it might be best to draw a curtain—is Mrs. Bennet, in the way she ends the sentence, drawing a curtain? If not, the sentence is constructed as a kind of trick, in the manner of a certain genre of ribald songs, to lead the listener to expect a guilty outcome and then disappoint that expectation with a perfectly innocent conclusion. Note, too, the possible play on the words "honest woman": an "honest woman" is one who confesses "the plain truth" of her desires, not a hypocrite obsessed with her "honesty."[13]

The events surrounding Mrs. Bennet's seduction are even more open to unfavorable interpretation. She hears favorably Mrs. Ellison ridicule conjugal love. She goes to a masquerade, where her "mind threw off all reserve, and pleasure only filled my thoughts," and she is "intoxicated with foolish desires, and liable to every temptation." When she meets the lord, she is "delighted with perceiving a passion in him," and even gives this passion "some very distant encouragement"—all of which she conceives to be within the bounds of innocence! She "draws the curtain" over her fall, in part perhaps because it would put her in no better light than the preceding events. Our least flattering interpretation is confirmed by Mrs. Bennet's conduct at the second masquerade.

Yet Mrs. Bennet is not presented as a villainous or evil person. In general, she is kind and helpful. She does

Amelia an inestimable service at the expense of revealing her own transgression. There can be little doubt that she later deeply regrets her seduction by the lord. Her devotion to both her husbands is apparent, and she describes the illness and death of her first husband as a devastating tragedy. She treats Atkinson with great fondness, and has "two fine boys, of whom they are equally fond."

This brief analysis of Mrs. Bennet has attempted to uncover only the most obvious complexities in her character, but it suggests that she is a remarkable creation for Henry Fielding. She embodies both good and evil, and we can see them battling in her. We see her less worthy inclinations—her ambition and selfishness—in the ascendancy, but we also see her warm, good nature prevail. In short, Mrs. Bennet emerges as a morally complex, ambiguous figure, and the high order of this achievement has best been stated by Coolidge.

> That such a character holds together, producing a recognizable, unified, personal image, is an achievement of a different kind from the conservation of character in *Tom Jones*. The character of Mrs. Atkinson seems the product of a more thoroughgoing, in a sense a less controlled, process of imagination than Fielding had hitherto ventured upon. In that process he develops a conception of the relationship between good and evil in human life which challenges that represented by his Amelia. He shows good will—the will to good—painfully struggling not so much to exclude evil as to get the better of it. Amelia's and Mrs. Atkinson's attitudes toward Mrs. Ellison, once that lady's activity has been made clear to both of them, are revelatory. For Amelia she is now simply a figure of evil; Mrs. Atkinson is willing both to find good in her and to put her to good use.[14]

A number of other characters in *Amelia* are presented with varying degrees of the same moral realism as Mrs. Bennet. Although Booth is basically a good man, at various times in his life he has been an irresponsible gambler, an adulterer, and an atheist—faults more serious than Tom Jones's lack of prudence. Mrs. Ellison may be a pimp, but she is not a heartless one; she makes certain that Mrs. Bennet receives a modest annuity from her cousin after he has done with her. Colonel James acts from a wide range of motives, which vary from good to indifferent to villainous. Even the minor figures sometimes lead credibly ambiguous moral lives. In wartime, Mr. Trent is a bold soldier, but when the war is over he becomes a deceitful procurer.

Fielding's final disregard for the moral complexity of these figures is certainly one of his least fortunate decisions in *Amelia*. Abandoning his fidelity to human experience as a changing moral phenomenon, which has hitherto guided his characterization, he mechanically reconciles plot to characters in the final chapter, punishing and rewarding the latter on the basis of a morally stereotyped classification that is at odds with their actions. His early beliefs about the nature of character again become operative, but because they are not compatible with his more recent conceptions, Fielding's characterization is revealed as contradictory and inconsistent.

III

If Fielding's achievement in the creation and presentation of Mrs. Bennet is as significant as Coolidge suggests, the question arises: Why are most of the other characters in the novel not equally successful, since the same new techniques are used to present them? One reason for the relative failure of these other characters is suggested by their "genealogy," inasmuch as most of the important characters in *Amelia* are direct descendants of figures in earlier Fielding novels. Amelia is a development of Sophia, who in turn is a development of Mrs. Heartfree through Fanny Goodwill. One basic character type, perhaps best expressed in Fanny's significant name, stands behind *all* these figures. Booth has been called an older, weaker, and less wise Tom Jones, and I think we can say he is also an older Joseph Andrews and Thomas Heartfree, for all three men are variations of Fielding's concept of the benevolent man. Dr. Harrison is a somewhat cynical Squire Allworthy, who is a development of Parson Adams. Miss Matthews is a variation on the woman of pleasure, seen earlier in Lady Bellaston, Lady Booby, and Laetitia Snap. But Mrs. Bennet has no previous model.[15]

Behind most of the principal people in *Amelia*, at least implicitly, are established stereotypes who were conceived in intensely intellectual and comic milieus but have now been transplanted to grave, sentimental milieus. Although Fielding is working with new techniques and experimental theories of characterization, he seems inhibited by his older conception of character because he did not abandon his traditional cast of people. Moreover, the new techniques are neither suitable nor adequate for presenting Fielding's earlier type characters. The novelist does not entirely succeed in escaping the limitations of his type characters, and he fails to achieve most of the advantages made available by his new approach. Booth, for example, emerges only implicitly as a type, yet he is one of the most improbable candidates for change, so that his conversion is forced and mechanical. This technical and conceptual confusion, this hybrid approach to character, lies behind the failure of *Amelia*'s figures to appear either as well defined as Fielding's earlier personages or as subtle and unique as Richardson's.

If Fielding's break with tradition was not complete or revolutionary in *Amelia*, it was nevertheless momentous, and the contrast between his early and late characterization is a remarkable antithesis. Relying completely on classical forms and literary devices for characterization, the novelist moved from this dependence to the virtual absence of such conventions in *Amelia*. And the characters also change in a manner that parallels this technical development. In his early novels, Fielding's figures are ethical embodiments of an absolute, intellectualized morality; in *Amelia*, his characters are representatives of a sentimental moral vision. In the comic romance, the ideals behind the figures are aristocratic; in *Amelia* the ideals are bourgeois. Few other eighteenth-century writers exemplify such a transformation.

Conclusions

𝕿HE ROOTS of Fielding's portraiture, this study contends, are to be found in both the classical and the earlier native and continental literary genres. The biographical character sketch, the idealized literary portrait, the emblematic portrait, and the literary caricature are forms that Fielding derived and adapted from descriptive traditions in classical writing and from French and English works. Contrary to what one might expect, however, the Theophrastan sketch, strictly understood—the classical genre usually believed to be highly relevant to the novelist's characterization—is not as germane as has commonly been imagined. Fielding's use of characteristic Theophrastan methods does not extend much beyond his portrayal of two figures, Thwackum and Square. For most of his psychological characterization he relied on techniques employed by the English character writers of the seventeenth century.

Using all these established descriptive modes, Fielding created his figures from his personal vision of the world. Unlike Samuel Richardson, who—as Morris Golden convincingly argues—manufactured his personages from his subjective sexual fantasies and cloaked these imaginings in an imposed ethical system,[1] Henry Fielding, fundamentally and naturally, was a moralist. He created his characters from his deeply and consciously held ethical and intellectual conceptions about human nature. Each figure in his novels is a rational actor, chosen with a specific purpose in mind, and together they form *schema* that examine different aspects of a central moral question.

As we would expect, the usual means by which the nature of these characters is defined (*i.e.*, the literary portraits) have an important place in the novels. The received wisdom about Fielding's characterization is that, in all his novels, dialogue and action are his most important means of revealing character. The findings of this study, of course, dispute that claim, and particularly as it pertains to his first three novels. Literary portraiture, more than any other technique, "fixes" character and establishes the nature and function of Fielding's figures in his early works.[2] Moreover, in addition to serving as "poetical embellishments" and rich sources of intellectual comedy, Fielding's portraits are among his most subtle instruments of theme.

Henry Fielding published his first novel in 1742 and his last one in 1751. During the interim his characterization underwent a gradual change. In general, this development parallels the changes in the literature and the intellectual tone or *zeitgeist* of the middle and late eighteenth century.[3] Fielding's early depiction used inherited aesthetic forms and presented character as a finished product. His later novels are marked by the gradual, and ultimately the complete, disappearance of classical methods of delineation and by the introduction of techniques that describe character as a process or a developing psychological phenomenon. There are also parallel changes in his characters. Figures change from embodiments of Field-ing's ironic intellectual viewpoint to representations of his domestic tragicomic vision.[4] At the same time, satire and comedy are withdrawn from the heroes and heroines (compare the portraits of Joseph and Tom) and become associated with minor figures.

In all its forms, literary portraiture plays a vital role in Fielding's characterization in his novels. The idealized portraits serve as highly functional set-piece literary ornaments. The caricatures, a principal source of comic irony in the novels, are the most vivid and memorable "pictures" of their kind in eighteenth-century literature. However, the greatest use of Fielding's observations on human nature is found in his direct character sketches. Among his most important methods of characterization, these sketches are his principal ethical medium and con-tain his most penetrating analyses of moral, social, and psychological patterns of human behavior.

Notes

NOTES TO THE INTRODUCTION

1. *Shamela* is not considered here; an epistolary travesty, it is an "engraftment" on Richardson's *Pamela*, not an independent work. Employing Richardson's epistolary style, it has no literary portraits as the term is understood in this study. Its characters are derived by means of confession and statements of intent that exploit ambiguities in Richardson's original.

2. B. W. Bates, *Literary Portraiture in the Historical Narrative of the French Renaissance* (New York, 1945), p. 2.

3. W. L. Cross, *The History of Henry Fielding* (New Haven, 1918), 2: 168–170; F. Holmes Dudden, *Henry Fielding* (Oxford, 1952), 2: 646–649; Miriam Allott, "A Note on Fielding's Mr Square," *MLR*, 56 (1961): 69–72.

4. W. G. Crane, *Wit and Rhetoric in the Renaissance* (New York, 1937), p. 154.

5. Michael Irwin, *Henry Fielding: The Tentative Realist* (Oxford, 1967), p. 51.

6. Even here the point can be made that many of these figures enter the drama from the character books.

7. Sheldon Sacks, *Fiction and the Shape of Belief* (Berkeley, 1964), p. 94.

8. G. E. Hammond, "Evidences of the Dramatist's Tech-

nique in Henry Fielding's Novels," *University Studies*, 16 (Wichita, 1941): 11.

9. There is such a study for one of Fielding's novels, J. R. De Bruyn's unpublished dissertation: "*Tom Jones:* A Genealogical Approach, Fielding's Use of Type Characters in *Tom Jones*" (New York University, 1954).

10. Robert M. Lovett and Helen S. Hughes, *The History of the Novel in England* (New York, 1932), p. 67.

11. George Saintsbury, *The English Novel* (London, 1913), p. 102.

12. W. L. Cross, *The Development of the English Novel* (New York, 1899), p. 57.

13. Ibid., p. 53.

14. Ibid., p. 46.

15. Ernest Baker, *The History of the English Novel* (London, 1930), 4: 149.

16. Ibid., p. 97.

17. The works of these scholars are cited in the bibliography at the end of this study.

NOTES TO CHAPTER ONE

1. Benjamin Boyce, *The Theophrastan Character in England to 1641* (Cambridge, Mass., 1947); Crane, *Wit and Rhetoric.*

2. *Wilson's Arte of Rhetorique*, ed. G. H. Mair (Oxford, 1909), p. 11.

3. F. R. Johnson, "Two Renaissance Textbooks of Rhetoric: Aphthonius' *Progymnasmata* and Rainolde's *A booke called the Foundacion of Rhetorike*," *HLQ*, 6 (1943): 427–444.

4. Boyce, *The Theophrastan Character*, p. 41.

5. Richard Rainolde, *The Foundacion of Rhetorike*, ed. Francis R. Johnson (New York, 1945), fol. xl.

6. Quoted in William J. Farrell's "The Mock-Heroic Form of *Jonathan Wild*," *MP*, 63 (1966): 226. My infor-

mation on Vicars's work comes from Farrell's article.

7. Charles W. Jones, *Saints' Lives and Chronicles in Early England* (Ithaca, 1947), p. 73; Donald A. Stauffer, *English Biography before 1700* (Cambridge, Mass., 1930), pp. 4–6.

8. Jones, *Saints' Lives and Chronicles*, p. 59.

9. O. B. Hardison, *The Enduring Monument* (Chapel Hill, 1962), p. 71.

10. I am indebted to Farrell's article (cited above) for many of the ideas of this paragraph.

11. Robert M. Wallace, "Fielding's Knowledge of History and Biography" *SP*, 44 (1947): 100.

12. Ibid., p. 90.

13. Donald A. Stauffer, *The Art of Biography in Eighteenth Century England* (Princeton, 1941), p. 92.

14. Sarah Fielding, *David Simple,* ed. Malcolm Kelsall (New York, 1969), p. 7.

15. Crane, *Wit and Rhetoric*, p. 154.

16. For much of this analysis of character traditions I am indebted to Boyce's work (cited above) and to "Theophrastus and His Imitators," in *English Literature and the Classics*, ed. George S. Gordon (Oxford, 1912).

17. I have used Johnson's book because it is so close to Fielding's time and because it was so popular. Five editions appeared between its publication in 1665 and the end of the century.

18. Quoted in *Collected Studies by Chester Noyes Greenough* (Cambridge, Mass., 1940), pp. 123–124.

19. These conceits are reserved for Fanny and Sophia.

20. *Encyclopaedia Britannica*, 11th ed., 2: 94–96.

21. This "Poeti Graeci," presumably, was the ancestor of *The Greek Anthology as Selected for the Use of Westminster, Eton, and Other Public Schools,* trans. George Burges (London, 1881).

22. Cross, *Henry Fielding*, 1: 44.

23. Ibid., pp. 44–45.

24. Item 603 in the sale catalogue of Fielding's library.

This catalogue was published in E. M. Thornbury's *Henry Fielding's Theory of the Comic Prose Epic* (Madison, 1931).

25. M. B. Ogle, "The Classical Origin and Tradition of Literary Conceits," *AJP*, 34 (1913): 125–152. This useful article indicates how widespread these conventions were.

26. *The Greek Anthology*, trans. W. R. Paton (London, 1927), 1: 191.

27. Fielding himself claimed that he formed his style on Lucian's, and what Dudden says of Fielding's *A Journey from this World to the Next* seems to be true of the influence of this portrait on the novelist's work: "He adopted a number of Lucian's ideas, but ingeniously translated them into contemporary, English forms, such as would be understood by, and afford amusement to, an eighteenth-century English reader" (Dudden, 1: 431).

28. Lucian, *Works*, trans. H. W. Fowler and F. G. Fowler (Oxford, 1905), 3: 16–23.

29. Edmond Faral, *Les Arts Poétiques du XIIᵉ et du XIIIᵉ Siècle* (Paris, 1923), pp. 79–81. Faral quotes a text to explain the rationale for the order of description in idealized portraiture, and, according to his source, nature, under the guidance of God, begins the creation of men with the head and proceeds downward to the feet.

30. Bill C. West, "Anti-Petrarchism: A Study of the Reaction against the Courtly Tradition in English Love-Poetry from Wyatt to Donne," unpublished dissertation, Northwestern University (1950), p. 35, n. 2.

31. The best analysis I have found of this topic is Ruth Kelso's *Doctrine for the Lady of the Renaissance* (Urbana, 1956), and I am particularly indebted to her chapter on love and beauty. Lu Emily Pearson's *Elizabethan Love Conventions* (Berkeley, 1933), Julius W. Lever's *The Elizabethan Love Sonnet* (London, 1956), Lisle Cecil John's *The Elizabethan Sonnet Sequences* (New York, 1938), and Walter Clyde Curry's *The Middle English Ideal of Personal Beauty* (Baltimore, 1916) have also been very helpful.

32. Madelein de Scudéry, *Almahide: or, the Captive Queen. An Excellent New Romance, Never before in English* (London, 1677), part 1, p. 11.

33. Quoted in Ogle, "Origin and Tradition of Literary Conceits," p. 125. Pearson refers to Watson's work as the "summary of all the exaggerated conventions of Petrarchism at this time in England" (Pearson, *Elizabethan Love Conventions*, p. 76).

34. Quoted in Lever, *Elizabethan Love Sonnet*, pp. 123–124.

35. See Ruth Kelso, "Love and Beauty," and Lu Emily Pearson, "Love and the Ideal Courtier," ch. 1, sec. 6.

36. Scudéry, *Almahide*, part 1, p. 57.

37. Ibid., p. 180.

38. M. B. Ogle, "Classical Literary Tradition in Early German and Romance Literature" *MLN*, 27 (1912): 242.

39. Jean H. Hagstrum, *The Sister Arts* (Chicago, 1958), pp. 224, 246.

40. Ibid., pp. 157–158.

41. Ibid., p. 12.

42. Jean H. Hagstrum, "Cariactures Verbal and Visual: or the Art of Distortion in the Age of Pope," unpublished lecture given 16 March 1968, Indiana University, p. 26.

43. R. E. Moore, *Hogarth's Literary Relationships* (Minneapolis, 1948), pp. 108–151.

44. Hagstrum, "Caricatures Verbal and Visual," p. 15.

45. E. H. Gombrich and E. Kris, *Caricature* (Harmondsworth, 1940), p. 13.

46. John Graham, "The Development of the Use of Physiognomy in the Novel," unpublished dissertation, Johns Hopkins University (1960), pp. 80–100.

NOTES TO CHAPTER TWO

1. Sacks, *Fiction and the Shape of Belief*, p. 8.

2. Henry Fielding, *Miscellanies* (London, 1743), 1: xxvi (quotations from the preface to *Jonathan Wild* are taken from this edition).

3. Charles O. McDonald, *The Rhetoric of Tragedy* (Amherst, Mass., 1966), p. 10.

4. Rainolde, *Foundacion of Rhetorike*, fol. xl.

5. I am indebted to William J. Farrell's article on *Jonathan Wild* (cited earlier) both here and below.

6. Farrell, "Mock-Heroic Form," p. 225.

7. Raymond Smith, "The Ironic Structure of Fielding's *Jonathan Wild*," *BSUF*, 6 (1965): 5.

8. J. E. Wells, "Fielding's Political Purpose in *Jonathan Wild*," *PMLA*, 21 (1913): 20.

9. A search of family and first names reveals no trace of "Marybone"; however, the following entry from Eilert Ekwall's *The Concise Oxford Dictionary of Place-Names* (Oxford, 1960 [p. 317]) seems relevant: "Marybone . . . Originally TYBURN, later altered to *Maryborne* . . . and by popular etymology to *Marylebone*."

10. The attitude to Alexander expressed in Fielding's poem "Of True Greatness" is representative:

> But hadst thou, *Alexander*, wish'd to prove
> Thy self the real Progeny of *Jove*,
> Virtue another Path had bid thee find,
> Taught thee to save, and not to slay Mankind.
>
> *Miscellanies*, 1: 5

11. William J. Farrell, "Fielding's Familiar Style," *ELH*, 34 (1967): 65–77.

12. Wells, "Political Purpose in *Jonathan Wild*," p. 32.

13. Ian Watt, *The Rise of the Novel* (Berkeley, 1965), pp. 279–280.

14. Those sentiments, suggestive of current thinking about *Jonathan Wild*, are representative of F. Holmes Dudden's judgments in his *Henry Fielding* (1: 487–491).

15. A. R. Humphreys, "Fielding's Irony: Its Methods and

Effects," in *Fielding: A Collection of Critical Essays*, ed. Ronald Paulson (Englewood Cliffs, 1962), p. 21.

16. Aurelien Digeon, *The Novels of Fielding* (New York, 1962), p. 225.

NOTES TO CHAPTER THREE

1. Martin Battestin, *The Moral Basis of Fielding's Art* (Middletown, Conn., 1959), p. 88.

2. Henry Fielding, *Joseph Andrews and Shamela*, ed. Martin Battestin (Boston, 1961), p. xxx.

3. See ch. 1, part 1, above.

4. Battestin, *Joseph Andrews and Shamela*, p. xxx.

5. Watt, *Rise of the Novel*, p. 281.

6. Dick Taylor, Jr., "Joseph as Hero in *Joseph Andrews*," *TSE*, 7 (1957): 91–109.

7. *Amelia* is an exception; see ch. 5 below.

8. See ch. 1 above.

9. R. P. Utter and G. B. Needham, *Pamela's Daughters* (New York, 1936), pp. 171–172.

10. R. E. Moore, *Hogarth's Literary Relationships*, p. 124.

11. *Oxford English Dictionary*.

12. *Three Books of Occult Philosophy*, ed. W. F. Whitehead (Chicago, 1898), p. 97.

13. J. T. McCullen, "Fielding's Beau Didapper," *ELN*, 2 (December 1964): 98–100.

14. The substance of these remarks is derived from the commentary on Didapper's sketch provided by Battestin's textual notes in the Wesleyan Fielding.

15. Battestin and Moore have commented on the use of Hogarth's material in Fielding's digression. Battestin's analysis has been of particular assistance to me.

16. William Hogarth, *Graphic Works*, ed. Paulson (New Haven, 1965), vol. 2, plate 138.

17. Sacks, *Fiction and the Shape of Belief*, p. 119.

18. Robert Alter, *Fielding and the Nature of the Novel* (Cambridge, Mass., 1968), p. 84.

19. Dudden, *Henry Fielding*, 1: 363.

20. Hagstrum, *The Sister Arts*, pp. 148–149.

21. Cesare Ripa, *Iconologia: or, Moral Emblems* (London, 1709), p. 37.

22. Douglas Brooks, "Abraham Adams and Parson Trulliber: The Meaning of *Joseph Andrews*, Book II, Chapter 14," *MLR*, 63 (October 1968): 794–801.

23. Quoted in Utter and Needham, *Pamela's Daughters*, p. 10.

24. It was Fielding's habit to think of elaborate descriptions in pictorial terms. In the context of a rather different subject, a landscape, he remarked: "The Soil was spread with a Verdure which no Paint could imitate" (*Joseph Andrews*, bk. 3, ch. 5).

25. Utter and Needham, *Pamela's Daughters*, p. 158. Gosse's work (Bibliography) reproduces this painting.

26. Slipslop is also praised by critics as a foil to Lady Booby.

27. Samuel Taylor Coleridge, *Biographia Literaria*, ed. Shawcross (London, 1962), 2: 102.

28. Ibid., p. 103.

NOTES TO CHAPTER FOUR

1. Sacks, *Fiction and the Shape of Belief*, pp. 110–192.

2. Dudden, *Henry Fielding*, 2: 619, 627.

3. Kettle, *The English Novel* (New York, 1960), p. 77.

4. A. R. Humphreys, "Fielding and Smollet," in *From Dryden to Johnson*, ed. Boris Ford (Baltimore, 1966), p. 320.

5. Battestin, *Fielding's Art*, p. 60.

6. Lynn C. Bartlett and William R. Sherwood, *The English Novel: Background Readings* (New York, 1967), p. 9.

7. Parson Adams is something of an exception to this rule.

The least allegorical of Fielding's paragons, he is described with some concreteness in *Joseph Andrews*. No mention of his appearance accompanies the initial sketch of his nature, as we have indicated; however, there are a few brief but vivid passages that describe his looks. They usually occur at points where the parson is involved in epic battles and where he is playing more the role of a comic figure than a paragon.

8. George Sherburn and Donald Bond, *The Restoration and the Eighteenth Century* (New York, 1967), p. 958.

9. André Gide, "Notes for a Preface to Fielding's *Tom Jones*," in *Fielding*, ed. Paulson (Englewood Cliffs, 1962), p. 82.

10. Dudden, *Henry Fielding*, 2: 645.

11. Alter, *The Nature of the Novel*, p. 85.

12. Sacks, *Fiction and the Shape of Belief*, pp. 141–150.

13. Quoted in Jean Hagstrum's *Samuel Johnson's Literary Criticism* (Chicago, 1967), p. 167.

14. Ian Watt, "Second Thoughts Series: Serious Reflections on *The Rise of the Novel*," *Novel*, 1 (1968): 215.

15. Irvin Ehrenpreis, *Tom Jones* (London, 1964), p. 73.

16. Digeon mentions the relevance of the first two figures but neglects the characters from *The Election*.

17. One difference between Allworthy and Square, suggested by the reference to Plato in this quote, is that while Square merely mouths Plato's ethical philosophy, Allworthy, a vital Christian, lives and acts it.

18. Samuel Johnson, *A Dictionary of the English Language* (London, 1799).

19. Fielding also uses the word "picture" in the sense of a "person, possessing a quality in so high a degree as to be a symbol or realization of that quality" *(OED)*, in order to identify Allworthy with benevolence.

20. Henry Knight Miller, *Essays on Fielding's Miscellanies* (Princeton, 1961), pp. 200–201.

21. This sentence may account for Fielding's description of Thwackum's countenance as resembling "that gentleman,

who in the Harlot's Progress is seen correcting the ladies in Bridewell." To emphasize the divine's sour nature, Fielding makes his face emblematic of his character by identifying him with a forbidding Hogarth figure. Fielding's reference to Hogarth's character cannot be taken as evidence (as Robert E. Moore suggests) that the engraver's print is the novelist's source for Thwackum. The labor-master is rather a vivid reference or equivalent and must be called a visual analogue, not a source.

22. Irwin, *Tentative Realist*, p. 94.

23. Andrew Wright, *Henry Fielding: Mask and Feast* (London, 1965), p. 163.

24. Ian Watt, "The Naming of Characters in Defoe, Richardson and Fielding," *RES*, 25 (1949): 335.

25. E. M. W. Tillyard, *The Epic Strain in the English Novel* (New York, 1958), p. 52.

26. Sheridan Baker, "Henry Fielding's Comic Romances," *PMASAL*, 45 (1960), 418.

27. Scudéry, *Almahide*, part 2, p. 63.

28. R. S. Crane, "The Plot of *Tom Jones*," *Journal of General Education*, 4 (1950): 112–130.

29. See plate 19B in *The Sister Arts*.

30. Ian Watt, "Second Thoughts Series," p. 217.

31. See plate 24 in *The Sister Arts*.

32. Ian Watt says: "Sophia never wholly recovers from so artificial an introduction, or at least never wholly disengages herself from the ironical attitude which it has induced" (*The Rise of the Novel*, pp. 254–255).

33. There are a number of these in the novel; bk. 10, ch. 5, opens this way.

34 C. J. Rawson, *Henry Fielding* (London, 1968), p. 27.

35. Martin Battestin, "Fielding's Definition of Wisdom," *ELH*, 35 (1968): 206.

36. For a graphic illustration of what the lord mayor's parade involved in Fielding's time, see Hogarth's *The Industrious Prentice Lord Mayor of London*.

37. "But tho' we have sometimes admitted this in our Diction, we have carefully excluded it from our Sentiments and Characters" (*Joseph Andrews*, preface).

38. Hagstrum, *The Sister Arts*, p. 313.

39. Rawson, *Henry Fielding*, p. 3, n. 20.

40. Hagstrum, *The Sister Arts*, p. 145.

41. Quoted in Battestin's "Fielding's Definition of Wisdom," p. 206.

42. Ibid., p. 206.

43. Ibid.

44. J. R. De Bruyn, *Tom Jones, DA*, 15 (1955), 1070.

45. It is virtually impossible to tell what visual analogue Fielding may have had in mind here. A *Diana* by Simon Vouet (1590–1649), believed to be commissioned by Charles I, was in Hampton Court at this time, and Fielding's references to Kneller's portraits suggest he may have been familiar with it. Ehrenpreis believes Fielding's figure is associated with the *Diana* in the Pantheon (Ehrenpreis, *Tom Jones*, p. 62).

46. Irwin, *Tentative Realist*, p. 109.

47. Martin Price, *To the Palace of Wisdom* (New York, 1965), p. 301.

48. Baker, *English Novel*, 4: 137.

49. Sheridan Baker, "Bridget Allworthy: The Creative Pressures of Fielding's Plot, *PMASAL*, 52 (1967): 348.

50. Ibid., p. 346.

51. R. E. Moore, *Hogarth's Literary Relationships*, p. 127.

NOTES TO CHAPTER FIVE

1. Sabine Nathan, "The Anticipation of Nineteenth-Century Ideological Trends in Fielding's *Amelia*," *ZAA*, 6 (1958): 402.

2. L. H. Powers, "The Influence of the *Aeneid* on Fielding's *Amelia*," *MLN*, 71 (1956): 331–332.

3. Paulson, *Hogarth's Graphic Works*, vol. 2, plate 148.

———— ◆●◆ ————

4. W. H. Stuart, "The Role of the Narrator in the Novels of Fielding," *DA*, 24 (1963): 2489–2490.

5. Ibid., p. 2490.

6. Henry Fielding, *The Covent-Garden Journal* (New Haven, 1915), 1: 186.

7. Digeon, *Novels of Fielding*, p. 84.

8. J. S. Coolidge, "Fielding and 'Conservation of Character,'" *Fielding*, ed. Paulson (New Jersey, 1962), p. 165. I am indebted to this article for pointing me in the general direction I have taken in this chapter as well as for a number of insights.

9. A. R. Humphreys in the introduction to his edition of *Amelia*, p. ix.

10. Dudden, *Henry Fielding*, 2: 837.

11. Watt, *The Rise of the Novel*, p. 20.

12. For a more detailed analysis of Mrs. Bennet see Coolidge, "Conservation of Character," pp. 158–176.

13. Ibid., p. 171.

14. Ibid., p. 175.

15. Most of these similarities have been noted by Baker in his *History of the English Novel* and, more recently, by Wright in *Henry Fielding: Mask and Feast*.

NOTES TO THE CONCLUSION

1. Morris Golden, *Richardson's Characters* (Ann Arbor, 1963).

2. Northrop Frye, "Towards Defining an Age of Sensibility," in *Eighteenth-Century English Literature*, ed. Clifford (New York, 1959), pp. 311–318.

3. Adams and Sophia are exceptions.

4. Morris Golden, *Fielding's Moral Psychology* (Amherst, Mass., 1966), p. 134.

Bibliography

PRIMARY SOURCES

Coleridge, Samuel Taylor. *Biographia Literaria*, ed. John Shawcross. 2 vols. London: Oxford University Press, 1962.

Fielding, Henry. *The Complete Works*, ed. William E. Henley. 16 vols. New York: Crosscup and Sterling, 1902.

———. *The Covent-Garden Journal*, ed. Gerard E. Jensen. 2 vols. New Haven: Yale University Press, 1915.

———. *Joseph Andrews*, ed. Martin Battestin. Middletown, Conn.: Wesleyan University Press, 1967.

———. *Joseph Andrews and Shamela*, ed. Martin Battestin. Boston: Houghton Mifflin, 1961.

———. *Miscellanies*. 3 vols. London: A. Millar, 1743.

———. *Tom Jones*, ed. R. P. C. Mutter. Baltimore: Penguin, 1966.

Fielding, Sarah. *The Adventures of David Simple*, ed. Malcoln Kelsall. New York: Oxford University Press, 1969.

The Greek Anthology, trans. W. R. Paton. 5 vols. London: W. Heinemann, 1917–1927.

The Greek Anthology as Selected for the Use of Westminster, Eton, and Other Public Schools, trans. George Burges. London: H. G. Bohn, 1881.

Hogarth, William. *Graphic Works*, ed. Ronald Paulson. 2 vols. New Haven: Yale University Press, 1965.

Bibliography

Johnson, Ralph. *The Scholars Guide from the Accidence to the University*. London, 1665.

Johnson, Samuel. *A Dictionary of the English Language*. London: T. N. Longman, 1799.

Lucian. *Works*, trans. H. W. Fowler and F. G. Fowler. 3 vols. Oxford: Clarendon Press, 1905.

Reynolds, Richard (Rainolde, Richard). *The Foundacion of Rhetorike*, ed. F. R. Johnson. New York: Scholars Facsimiles Reprints, 1945.

Ripa, Cesare. *Iconologia: or, Moral Emblems*. London: B. Motte, 1709.

Scudéry, Madelein de. *Almahide: or, the Captive Queen. An Excellent New Romance, Never before in English*. London: Thomas Dring, 1677.

Vicars, Thomas. *Manductio ad Artem Rhetoricana*. London, 1721.

Whitehead, W. F., ed. *Three Books of Occult Philosophy*. Chicago: Hahn and Whitehead, 1898.

[Wilson, Thomas]. *Wilson's Arte of Rhetorique*, ed. G. H. Mair. Oxford: Clarendon Press, 1909.

SECONDARY SOURCES

Allen, Walter. *The English Novel*. New York: E. P. Dutton, 1954.

Allott, Miriam. "A Note on Fielding's Mr Square," *MLR*, 56 (1961): 69–72.

Alter, Robert. *Fielding and the Nature of the Novel*. Cambridge, Mass.: Harvard University Press, 1968.

———. *The Rogue's Progress: Studies in the Picaresque Novel*. Cambridge, Mass.: Harvard University Press, 1964.

Amory, Hugh. "Law and the Structure of Fielding's Novels," *DA*, 27 (1966): 451A–452A.

Baker, Ernest A. *The History of the English Novel.* 10 vols. London: H. F. and G. Witherby, 1924–1939.

Baker, Sheridan. "Bridget Allworthy: The Creative Pressures of Fielding's Plot," *PMASAL*, 52 (1967): 345–356.

———. "Henry Fielding's Comic Romances," *PMASAL*, 45 (1960): 411–419.

Bartlett, Lynn C., and William R. Sherwood. *The English Novel: Background Readings.* New York: J. B. Lippincott, 1967.

Bates, B. W. *Literary Portraiture in the Historical Narrative of the French Renaissance.* New York: G. E. Stechert, 1945.

Battestin, Martin. "Fielding's Definition of Wisdom: Some Functions of Ambiguity and Emblem in *Tom Jones*," *ELH*, 35 (1968): 188–217.

———. *The Moral Basis of Fielding's Art.* Middletown, Conn.: Wesleyan University Press, 1959.

Bissell, Frederick O. *Fielding's Theory of the Novel.* Ithaca: Cornell University Press, 1933.

Boyce, Benjamin. *The Character-Sketches in Pope's Poems.* Durham, N.C.: Duke University Press, 1962.

———. *The Theophrastan Character in England to 1642.* Cambridge, Mass.: Harvard University Press, 1947.

Brooks, Douglas. "Abraham Adams and Parson Trulliber: The Meaning of *Joseph Andrews*, Book II, Chapter 14," *MLR*, 63 (1968): 794–801.

Clifford, James L., ed. *Eighteenth-Century English Literature: Modern Essays in Criticism.* New York: Oxford University Press, 1959.

Cooke, Arthur L. "Henry Fielding and the Writers of Heroic Romance," *PMLA*, 62 (1947): 984–994.

Crane, R. S. "The Plot of *Tom Jones*," *JGE*, 4(1950): 112–130.

Bibliography

Crane, W. G. *Wit and Rhetoric in the Renaissance*. New York: Columbia University Press, 1937.

Cross, Wilbur L. *The Development of the English Novel*. New York: Macmillan, 1899.

———. *The History of Henry Fielding*. 3 vols. New Haven: Yale University Press, 1918.

Curry, Walter Clyde. *The Middle English Ideal of Personal Beauty*. Baltimore: J. H. Furst, 1916.

De Bruyn, J. R. "*Tom Jones:* A Genealogical Approach, Fielding's Use of Type Characters in *Tom Jones*," *DA*, 15 (1955): 1070.

Digeon, Aurelien. *The Novels of Fielding*. New York: Russell and Russell, 1962.

Dircks, Richard J. " 'The Perils of Heartfree': A Sociological Review of Fielding's Adaptation of Dramatic Convention," *TSLL*, 8 (1966): 5–13.

Dudden, F. Holmes. *Henry Fielding, His Life, Works, and Times*. 2 vols. Oxford: Clarendon Press, 1952.

Ehrenpreis, Irvin. *Fielding: Tom Jones*. Studies in English Literature, No. 23. London: Edward Arnold, 1964.

Ekwall, Eilert. *The Concise Oxford Dictionary of English Place-Names*. Oxford: Clarendon Press, 1960.

Empson, William. "*Tom Jones*," *KR*, 20 (1958): 217–249.

Encyclopaedia Britannica. 11th ed. 29 vols. New York: Encyclopaedia Britannica, 1910.

Faral, Edmond. *Les Arts Poétiques du XIIᵉ et du XIIIᵉ Siècle*. Paris: E. Champion, 1924.

Farrell, William J. "Fielding's Familiar Style," *ELH*, 34 (1967): 65–77.

———. "The Mock-Heroic Form of *Jonathan Wild*," *MP*, 63 (1966): 216–226.

Ford, Boris, ed. *From Dryden to Johnson*. Baltimore: Penguin, 1966.

Golden, Morris. *Fielding's Moral Psychology*. Amherst, Mass.: University of Massachusetts Press, 1966.

———. *Richardson's Characters*. Ann Arbor: University of Michigan Press, 1963.

Gombrich, E. H., and E. Kris. *Caricature*. Harmondsworth: Penguin, 1940.

Gordon, George S., ed. *English Literature and the Classics*. Oxford: Clarendon Press, 1912.

Gosse, Edmund. *Peintres et Graveurs Anglais du XVIIIe Siècle*. Paris: Goupie, 1906.

Graham, John. "The Development of the Use of Physiognomy in the Novel." Unpublished dissertation, Johns Hopkins University, 1960.

[Greenough, Chester N.]. *Collected Studies by Chester Noyes Greenough*. Cambridge, Mass.: Merrymount Press, 1940.

Hagstrum, Jean H. "Caricatures Verbal and Visual: or The Art of Distortion in the Age of Pope." Unpublished lecture given at Indiana University, 16 March 1968.

———. *Samuel Johnson's Literary Criticism*. Chicago: University of Chicago Press, 1967.

———. *The Sister Arts: The Tradition of Literary Pictorialism and English Poetry from Dryden to Gray*. Chicago: University of Chicago Press, 1958.

Hammond, Geraldine E. "Evidences of the Dramatist's Technique in Henry Fielding's Novels," *University Studies*, 16 (Wichita, 1941): 3–27.

Hardison, O. B. *The Enduring Monument: A Study of the Idea of Praise in Renaissance Literary Theory and Practice*. Chapel Hill: University of North Carolina Press, 1962.

Irwin, Michael. *Henry Fielding: The Tentative Realist*. Oxford: Clarendon Press, 1967.

John, Lisle Cecil. *The Elizabethan Sonnet Sequences*. New York: Columbia University Press, 1938.

Johnson, F. R. "Two Renaissance Textbooks of Rhetoric: Aphthonius' *Progymnasmata* and Rainolde's *A Booke called the Foundacion of Rhetorike*," *HLQ*, 6 (1943): 427–444.

Jones, Charles W. *Saints' Lives and Chronicles in Early England.* Ithaca: Cornell University Press, 1947.

Kelso, Ruth. *Doctrine for the Lady of the Renaissance.* Urbana: University of Illinois Press, 1956.

Kettle, Arnold. *An Introduction to the English Novel.* 2 vols. New York: Harper and Row, 1960.

Kishler, Thomas C. "Heartfree's Function in *Jonathan Wild*," *Satire Newsletter*, 1 (1964): 32–34.

Lever, Julius W. *The Elizabethan Love Sonnet.* London: Methuen, 1956.

Levine, George R. *Henry Fielding and the Dry Mock: A Study of the Techniques of Irony in His Early Works.* The Hague: Mouton, 1967.

Lovett, Robert M., and Helen S. Hughes. *The History of the Novel in England.* New York: Houghton Mifflin, 1932.

McCullen, J. T. "Fielding's Beau Didapper," *ELN*, 2 (1964): 98–100.

McDonald, Charles O. *The Rhetoric of Tragedy.* Amherst, Mass.: University of Massachusetts Press, 1966.

Miller, Henry Knight. *Essays on Fielding's Miscellanies.* Princeton: Princeton University Press, 1961.

———. "Some Functions of Rhetoric in *Tom Jones*," *PQ*, 45 (1966): 209–235.

Moore, R. E. *Hogarth's Literary Relationships.* Minneapolis: University of Minnesota Press, 1948.

Nathan, Sabine. "The Anticipation of Nineteenth-Century Ideological Trends in Fielding's *Amelia*," *ZAA*, 6 (1958): 382–409.

Ogle, M. B. "The Classical Origin and Tradition of Literary Conceits," *AJP*, 34 (1913): 125-152.

Ogle, M. B. "Classical Literary Tradition in Early German and Romance Literature," *MLN*, 27 (1912): 233–242.

Paulson, Ronald, ed. *Fielding: A Collection of Critical Essays.* Englewood Cliffs: Prentice-Hall, 1962.

Pearson, Lu Emily. *Elizabethan Love Conventions.* Berkeley: University of California Press, 1933.

Powers, Lyall H. "The Influence of the *Aeneid* on Fielding's *Amelia,*" *MLN*, 71 (1956): 330–336.

Price, Martin. *To the Palace of Wisdom.* New York: Doubleday, 1965.

Rawson, C. J. *Profiles in Literature: Henry Fielding.* London: Routledge and Kegan Paul, 1968.

Roscoe, Adrian A. "Fielding and the Problem of Allworthy," *TSLL*, 7 (1965): 169–172.

Sacks, Sheldon. *Fiction and the Shape of Belief.* Berkeley: University of California Press, 1964.

Saintsbury, George. *The English Novel.* London: E. P. Dutton, 1913.

Sherburn, George, and Donald Bond. *The Restoration and the Eighteenth Century.* New York: Appleton-Century-Crofts, 1967.

Smith, Raymond. "The Ironic Structure of Fielding's *Jonathan Wild,*" *BSUF*, 6 (1965): 3–9.

Stauffer, Donald A. *The Art of Biography in Eighteenth Century England.* Princeton: Princeton University Press, 1941.

———. *English Biography before 1700.* Cambridge, Mass.: Harvard University Press, 1930.

Stuart, Walter H. "The Role of the Narrator in the Novels of Fielding," *DA*, 24 (1963): 2489–2490.

Taylor, Dick, Jr. "Joseph as Hero in *Joseph Andrews,*" *TSE*, 7 (1957): 91–109.

Thornbury, Ethel M. *Henry Fielding's Theory of the Comic*

Prose Epic. University of Wisconsin Studies in Language and Literature. Madison: University of Wisconsin Press, 1931.

Tieje, A. J. *The Theory of Characterization in Prose Fiction Prior to 1740.* Minneapolis: University of Minnesota Press, 1916.

Tillyard, E. M. W. *The Epic Strain in the English Novel.* New York: Oxford University Press, 1958.

Utter, R. P., and G. B. Needham. *Pamela's Daughters.* New York: Macmillan, 1936.

Wallace, Robert M. "Fielding's Knowledge of History and Biography," *SP*, 44 (1947): 89–107.

Watt, Ian P. "The Naming of Characters in Defoe, Richardson and Fielding," *RES*, 25 (1949): 322–338.

————. *The Rise of the Novel.* Berkeley: University of California Press, 1965.

————. "Second Thoughts Series: Serious Reflections on *The Rise of the Novel*," *Novel*, 1 (1968): 205–218.

Wells, J. E. "Fielding's Political Purpose in *Jonathan Wild*," *PMLA*, 21 (1913): 1–55.

Wendt, A. "The Moral Allegory of *Jonathan Wild*," *ELH*, 24 (1957): 306–320.

West, Bill C. "Anti-Petrarchism: A Study of the Reaction against the Courtly Tradition in English Love-Poetry from Wyatt to Donne." Unpublished dissertation, Northwestern University, 1950.

Wright, Andrew. *Henry Fielding: Mask and Feast.* London: Chatto and Windus, 1965.

Index

Aeneid (Virgil), 56, 158

Almahide (Scudéry), 31, 33–37, 127–28

Amelia (Fielding): Amelia, 169–70; 175; beauty as an index of character in, 163, 169–70; Blear-eyed Moll, 158–62; Booth, 168–69, 174, 175–76; character development in, 171–74, 175–76; didactic and sentimental tone of, 154, 155, 157, 158, 162; empirical approach in, 165–66; ending to the novel, 174; Harrison, 155, 175; James, 174; Mrs. Bennet, 167–68, 171–75; narrator in, 155, 157, 162, 164–65, 170; proper and common names in, 170–71; reformist purpose of, 154–55, 157–58, 163; stereotypes in, 175;

Thraser, 156–58; Trent, 174

Aphthonius, *Progymnasmata*, 12

Baker, Ernest, *The History of the English Novel*, 9, 143

Baker, Sheridan, 146

Battestin, Martin, 73, 89, 140

Beauty, standards of, 30, 78

Biographia Literaria (Coleridge), 101

Biographies, classical and contemporary, 14–15

Boucher, François, *Madame de Pompadour*, 96

Brooks, Douglas, 93

The Champion (Fielding), 15

Character presentation: allegorical and emblematic aspects to, 43–44, 81–83,

Character presentation
(*cont.*)

99–101, 108–9, 111; ana-
tomical catalogue in, 22,
24–25, 26–27, 31, 33–37,
42, 126–27, 138; color in,
22, 24–25, 27, 32, 138; decorum in, 97, 130, 166;
development of, 70–71,
102–5, 150–53, 176, 177–
79; idealization in, 25–26,
28, 41, 97, 130, 139–40;
names as a method of, 71,
89, 103, 124, 151, 157, 160,
170–71; pictorial qualities
in, 25–26, 38–40, 64–65,
69, 76–77, 95–97, 100, 101,
135, 136–39
*Characters of Vertues and
Vices* (Hall), 18
Coleridge, Samuel Taylor,
Biographia Literaria, 101
Coolidge, J. S., 173, 174
*The Covent-Garden Jour-
nal* (Fielding), 165
Crane, Ronald S., 129
Cross, Wilbur L., *Devel-
opment of the English
Novel,* 8

David Simple, preface
(Fielding), 6, 15–16
Decorum. *See* Character
presentation, decorum in
Dialogues (Lucian), 26–30
Diana (Vouet), 190*n* 45

*Dictionary of the English
Language* (Johnson), 117
Digeon, Aurelien, 165
Don Quixote in England
(Fielding), 112
Dudden, F. Holmes, 110–11,
170, 183*n* 27

The Election (Fielding),
112
"An Essay on Conversa-
tion" (Fielding), 114
"Essay on the Knowledge
of the Characters of
Men" (Fielding), 78–79,
109, 116, 119–20
Ethical patterns and con-
trasts in character draw-
ing, 20, 47, 59, 70, 104,
107, 111–12, 120–21, 140,
143–44, 150–51, 167
Eton College. *See* Fielding,
Henry, education at Eton

Farrell, William J., 50
Fielding, Henry: aesthetic
of, 5–6; attitude toward
hypocrisy, 54, 119, 121;
attitude toward religion,
113, 117, 119–20; attitude
toward sexuality, 78, 128–
29; class consciousness,
50, 73, 80, 88, 97, 102, 129,
149; conception of be-
nevolence, 61, 108–9,
112–14; dramatist, 7–8;
education at Eton, 12, 17,

23; ethical vision in his novels, 71, 103–5, 107, 109, 111–12, 150–51, 154–55, 160–61, 178; theory of physiognomy, 78–79, 98; William Hogarth, 159–61. Works: *Amelia*, 154–76; *The Champion*, 15; *The Covent-Garden Journal*, 165; *David Simple* (preface), 6, 15–16; *Don Quixote in England*, 112; *The Election*, 112; "An Essay on Conversation," 114; "Essay on the Knowledge of the Characters of Men," 78–79, 109, 116, 119–20; *Jonathan Wild*, 45–71; *Joseph Andrews*, 72–105; "Love in Several Masques," 112; *Shamela*, 180*n* 1; *Tom Jones*, 106–53, 188*n* 17, 188*n* 19

The Foundacion of Rhetorike (Reynolds), 12–13, 47–49

Gentleman's Magazine, 109
Gide, André, 110
Gombrich, E. H., and E. Kris, *Caricature*, 43
The Greek Anthology, 23–26, 29

Hagiography, 14, 49

Hagstrum, Jean H., 41
Hall, Joseph, *Characters of Vertues and Vices*, 18
Hervey, Lord John, 83–84
Histories. *See* Biographies
Hogarth, William, 39, 41, 84–88, 100, 159–61, 188*n* 21, 189*n* 36. Works: *A Harlot's Progress*, 85–86; *A Midnight Modern Conversation*, 87; *Morning*, 146–47; *Noon*, 81; *A Rake's Progress*, 85–88

Iconologia: or, Moral Emblems (Ripa), 43, 92
Idealization, artistic. *See* Character presentation, idealization in
Identifications with historical figures. *See* Real-life people as models
Institutes of Oratory (Quintilian), 12

Johnson, Ralph, *The Scholars Guide from the Accidence to the University*, 17–18
Johnson, Samuel, *Dictionary of the Englisb Language*, 117
Jonathan Wild (Fielding): Bagshot, 66, 68–69; Blueskin, 57–58; comic interest in, 69, 70, 71; Fireblood, 55–57; flat and

Jonathan Wild (cont.)
round characters in, 69–
71; form of, 45–46; good-
ness versus greatness, 45–
46, 60, 70; Marybone, 55;
minor versus major fig-
ures in, 69; as mock-
heroic biography, 49, 56;
Mr. Heartfree, 47, 58–61,
70; Mrs. Heartfree, 61;
political satire in, 50, 51,
54, 55, 56–57; purpose of,
45–46, 69; Smirk, 66–68;
Tishy, 64–66; Wild, 47–
55, 60–61, 70
Joseph Andrews (Field-
ing): Adams, 89–91,
187*n* 7; Beau Didapper,
80–84; concept of sim-
plicity in, 90–91; country
versus city in, 88–89;
digression in, 84–89; Fanny, 77–78, 93–97, 98;
Fielding describes his
character drawing in, 5–6;
Joseph, 73–80, 88–89;
nature and function of
characters in, 73; purpose
of, 72–73; Slipslop, 97–99;
"surprise" ending, 79–80;
Trulliber, 91–93; Tow-
wouse, 99–101; Wilson,
84–89

Kneller, Sir Godfrey, 136–
37

La belle nature. See Char-
acter presentation, ideal-
ization in
Laus et vituperatio. See
Praise and blame
Lely, Sir Peter, 137
Life of Cicero (Middleton),
14, 84
"Love in Several Masques"
(Fielding), 112
Lovett, Robert, and Helen
S. Hughes, *The History
of the Novel in England*,
8
Lucian: *Dialogues*, 26–30;
*Quomodo Historia Scrib-
enda Sit*, 62

Madame de Pompadour
(Boucher), 96
*Manductio ad Artem Rhe-
toricana* (Vicars), 13
Middleton, Conyers, *Life of
Cicero*, 14, 84
Miller, Henry Knight, 119
Moore, R. E., *Hogarth's
Literary Relationships*,
146, 160

*A New World of English
Words* (Phillips), 99

Ogle, M. B., 38

Pamela, (Richardson), 94,
95

Phillips, Edward, *A New World of English Words*, 99

Phoebus and the Hours, Preceded by Aurora (Reni), 135

Physiognomy, Fielding's theory of. *See* Fielding, Henry, theory of physiognomy

Plato, 114

Poeti Graeci. See The Greek Anthology

Pope, Alexander, 5, 83

Portrait of a Lady with an Ermine (Vinci), 100

Portraiture, literary: biographical character sketch, 10–15, 47–50, 70–71, 73–74, 102, 108, 150; decline of, 151–53, 164–67; defined, 3–4; English character sketch, 16–19, 51–55, 130; functions of, 6, 63; idealized portraiture, 20–40, 65–66, 67, 75–78, 94–97, 125–28, 183*n* 29; portrait caricature, 40–44, 80–81, 98–101, 149; set-piece characterization, 4, 151; Theophrastan character sketch, 16–17, 118, 177

Praise and blame, the formula for, 11–14, 49–50, 73–74

Progymnasmata (Aphthonius), 12

Quintilian, *Institutes of Oratory*, 12

Quomodo Historia Scribenda Sit (Lucian), 62

Rainolde, Richard. *See* Reynolds, Richard

Rawson, C. J., 137

Real-life people as models, 5–6, 83–84

Reni, Guido, *Phoebus and the Hours, Preceded by Aurora*, 135

Reynolds, Richard, *The Foundacion of Rhetorike*, 12–13, 47–49

Reynolds, Sir Joshua, 137, 138

Rhetoric books, the influence of, 11–14, 17–18, 29, 47–50

Richardson, Samuel, 8, 80, 94, 177–78

Ripa, Cesare, *Iconologia: or, Moral Emblems*, 43, 92

Rochester. *See* Wilmot, John

Sacks, Sheldon, 111

Saintsbury, George, *The English Novel*, 8

The Scholars Guide from the Accidence to the University (Johnson), 17–18

Scudéry, Madelein de, *Al-mahide*, 31, 33–37, 127–128

Shamela (Fielding), 180*n* 1

Sherburn, George, 110

Sherry, Richard, *A Treatise of Schemes and Tropes*, 12

Spectator, 14, 18–19

Spence, Joseph, 139

Spenser, Edmund, 32

Theophrastus, 17, 71, 118

Tom Jones (Fielding): Allworthy, 107–11, 112, 116–18, 120–21, 155, 188*n* 7, 188*n* 19; Bridget Allworthy, 144–47; Blifil, 120–24; Captain Blifil, 147–50; Di Western, 140–43; Lady Bellaston, 143–44; Mrs. Waters, 127–29; Sophia, 130–40; Thwackum and Square, 112–20; Tom, 120–31; Western, 112, 120, 139, 140–41

Trapp, Joseph, 111

A Treatise of Schemes and Tropes (Sherry), 12

Venus and Adonis, 25–26, 129–130

Venus dei Medici, 25, 130, 136, 138–39

Vicars, Thomas, *Manductio ad Artem Rhetoricana*, 14

Vinci, Leonardo da, *Portrait of a Lady with an Ermine*, 100

Virgil, *Aeneid*, 56, 158

Visual arts. *See* Character presentation, pictorial qualities in

Vouet, Simon, *Diana*, 190*n* 45

Walpole, Robert, 50, 54

Watson, Thomas, 31–32

Watt, Ian, 189*n* 32

Wilmot, John, 137

Wilson, Thomas, *Wilson's Arte of Rhetorique*, 11–12